NAFTA at Three

Significant Issues Series

SIGNIFICANT ISSUES SERIES papers are written for and published by the Center for Strategic and International Studies.

Director of Studies: Erik R. Peterson

Director of Publications: James R. Dunton

Managing Editor: Roberta L. Howard

The Center for Strategic and International Studies (CSIS), established in 1962, is a private, tax-exempt institution focusing on international public policy issues. Its research is nonpartisan and nonproprietary.

CSIS is dedicated to policy analysis and impact. It seeks to inform and shape selected policy decisions in government and the private sector to meet the increasingly complex and difficult global challenges that leaders will confront in the next century. It achieves this mission in three ways: by generating strategic analysis that is anticipatory and interdisciplinary; by convening policymakers and other influential parties to assess key issues; and by building structures for policy action.

CSIS does not take specific public policy positions. Accordingly, all views, positions, and conclusions expressed in this publication should be understood to be solely those of the authors.

❖   ❖   ❖

The Center for Strategic and International Studies
1800 K Street, N.W.
Washington, D.C.   20006
Telephone: (202) 887-0200
Fax: (202) 775-3199
E-mail: info@csis.org
Web site: http://www.csis.org/

NAFTA at Three
A Progress Report

Sidney Weintraub

Foreword by *Julius Katz*

THE CENTER FOR STRATEGIC & INTERNATIONAL STUDIES
Washington, D.C.

Significant Issues Series, Volume XIX, Number 1
© 1997 by The Center for Strategic and International Studies
Washington, D.C. 20006

99   98   5   4

ISSN 0736-7136
ISBN 0-89206-298-3

Library of Congress Cataloging-in-Publication Data

Weintraub, Sidney, 1922–
   NAFTA at three : a progress report / by Sidney Weintraub ;
   foreword by Julius L. Katz.
       p.   cm. — (Significant issues series, ISSN 0736-7136 ; v. 19, no. 1)
   ISBN 0-89206-298-3
       1. Canada. Treaties, etc. 1992 Oct. 7.   2. Free trade—North
   America.   3. Free trade—Mexico.   4. North America—Foreign
   economic relations.   5. Mexico—Economic conditions—1994–
   I. Katz, Julius L.   II. Title.   III. Series
HF176.W438   1997
382′.917--dc21   97-1941
                                                            CIP

Contents

6
Conclusions   83

Foreword

The conclusion of NAFTA was one of the more significant achievements of U.S. trade policy in the past 50 years. It was at the same time a highly controversial trade policy development. An assessment of its results after only three years, as the author notes, must necessarily be preliminary. Yet a review is now timely for several reasons. Although NAFTA did not figure importantly in the 1996 election campaign, the direct attacks by Ross Perot, and his running mate, and the doubts raised by Senator Dole went mostly unanswered by President Clinton. With the campaign out of the way, a more balanced evaluation may now be possible.

A review is also timely because the Congress is likely to consider new "fast-track" legislation to permit negotiations to admit Chile and possibly others to the NAFTA. It will almost certainly want to examine how NAFTA is faring.

Finally, under the NAFTA legislation the president is required to provide a comprehensive study to the Congress by July 1, 1997 on the operation and effects of the agreement. The terms of reference for this report specified in the law reflect what Sidney Weintraub refers to as the "unadulterated mercantilism" employed by the Clinton administration to gain congressional support for the agreement. The effects of the agreement on the U.S. gross national product, employment, balance of trade, specific industries (including wages and productivity), and investment flows are among the factors to be assessed in the president's report.

As Weintraub points out, these are not the most appropriate criteria by which to evaluate the effects of the agreement. He notes that NAFTA is a framework for bilateral economic relations and not a dominant factor in the internal economies of the countries. Because of the huge disparity in size of the U.S. and Mexican economies—Mexico's is one-twentieth (and Canada's one-tenth) that of the United States—the influence of NAFTA on the U.S. economy is minimal at best. That is not to say that there is no impact on individual firms and communities, but even this effect must be viewed in the larger context of the world marketplace.

It is unfortunate that the worth of NAFTA came to be viewed largely in terms of the trade balance and jobs. The author has labeled these arguments as "95 percent rubbish." These were not the primary considerations that led the Bush administration to decide in 1990 to undertake the NAFTA negotiations.

While the public rhetoric of the Bush administration in support of free trade negotiations with Mexico, like that of the Clinton administration, spoke of exports and jobs, this was in reaction to the charge by the AFL-CIO that an agreement with Mexico would result in massive job losses for the United States. In internal deliberations, however, the Bush administration saw an agreement with Mexico as an element of a broader trade strategy that sought to promote free trade throughout the Western Hemisphere and provide a stimulus for multilateral trade negotiations.

An agreement with Mexico also was seen as a means of giving support for the economic reforms of the Salinas administration, which the U.S. administration believed would promote economic growth and greater cooperation between the two governments on matters of mutual interest such as drugs and immigration.

The major contribution of this progress report is to provide a more multifaceted balance sheet with which to assess NAFTA, more appropriate than the narrow focus on exports and jobs. Rejecting the automatic relationship between exports and jobs, the author points out that an analysis of the jobs issue requires a more complex inquiry than merely measuring net exports. Just as exports do not automatically equate with job growth, imports do not automatically equate with job losses. Imports of oil and other needed goods, for example, do not mean a loss of jobs. Similarly, imports of components may be tied to exports of finished goods and contribute to overall export competitiveness.

After examining the "wrong" criteria for assessing NAFTA, Weintraub discusses what he regards as the more salient criteria that should be used with respect to the U.S. relationship with Mexico. Among these are growth in total trade, not merely exports; the promotion of intra-industry trade and specialization; and the effects on productivity and wages, on the competitive position of industries, on the environment, and, finally, on institution building. I agree that this is an appropriate array of interests that should be examined in any assessment of NAFTA. Of these issues, only the environmental issue was not among the objectives initially contemplated by the Bush administration when the idea of a free trade negotiation with Mexico was first discussed in 1990.

Weintraub observes that Mexico and the United States were drawn kicking and screaming into linking trade and the environment by the insistence of environmental groups. When the link between trade and the environment and labor became issues in the fast-track debate in 1991, President Bush and his negotiators explicitly committed to the congressional leadership that the negotiations would include both issues. During the course of the negotiations, the environmental ministers met on numerous occasions, both with and without the trade ministers, and agreed on a range of environmental and labor commitments. A Memorandum of Understanding signed in May 1992 provided for closer cooperation and joint action on a range of labor issues over a five-year period, including projects in the areas of occupational health and safety, child labor, labor statistics, labor law, and worker rights.

On environmental policy, the United States and Mexico agreed in February 1992 on an integrated border plan intended, among other things, to strengthen enforcement of environmental laws, to reduce pollution through a number of joint initiatives, and to spend more than $1 billion on border air, water, and sewage projects.

In addition to the parallel arrangements, NAFTA itself contains several provisions dealing directly with the issue of the environment. NAFTA chapters on standards and on sanitary and phytosanitary measures were drawn to preserve the ability of the parties to the agreement to maintain strong health, safety, and environmental standards. The parties also agreed to give priority to several international environmental and conservation agreements in the event of any inconsistency between NAFTA and these international agreements. They also agreed that they would not relax environmental standards as a means to attract investment. The dispute-settlement chapter is intended to support environmental policy by placing the burden of proof on those challenging the consistency of an environmental measure with the agreement. Further, there is provision for convening an independent scientific review board on issues of fact concerning the environment, health, or safety. The treatment of environmental issues in NAFTA persuaded a number of major environmental groups to endorse the agreement.

Under the prodding of more radical environmental groups, as well as the AFL-CIO, President Clinton took the position that the NAFTA provisions on the environment and the parallel arrangements on labor and the environment were inadequate. He insisted on new side agreements, which contain the possibility of sanctions in the event a participating government fails to enforce its domestic laws and regulations in the areas covered by the agreements.

I would note finally that the Clinton administration has paid a price for having forced the Mexicans and Canadians to accept its side agreements. That price has been the unwillingness of the

Congress to renew fast-track negotiating authority in a form that would permit future agreements to use trade sanctions to enforce labor and environmental standards. Thus, the expectation that NAFTA would be expanded to include Chile and perhaps other countries has been frustrated so far. This was an unfortunate and unintended effect of the Clinton side agreements.

JULIUS L. KATZ
President, Hills & Company
Former Deputy U.S. Trade Representative

Acknowledgments

Because I live in Washington, D.C., I have ready access to many officials intimately engaged in making U.S. trade policy and am in regular contact with the many experts in this city who analyze and comment on what the policymakers do. These analysts are from the private and public sectors, from business, universities, and think tanks. My position at the Center for Strategic and International Studies enables me to discuss NAFTA and other trade issues with interested members of the U.S. Congress. My most important acknowledgments go to all these interlocutors. They are too numerous to list here.

Officials of the Mexican embassy in Washington also have provided their government's viewpoint on NAFTA issues, as have the responsible officials in Mexico City during my frequent visits. I stay in regular contact with nongovernmental analysts in Mexico. I owe much of my sense of how Mexicans see the effects of NAFTA to these conversations.

I am particularly grateful to Professor Chandler Stolp of the Lyndon B. Johnson School of Public Affairs of the University of Texas at Austin and to Jules Katz, both of whom read the final draft manuscript and made valuable suggestions. Most of these have been incorporated in the final publication. Jules, based on his long experience in trade policy as a government official—and a key negotiator of NAFTA during the administration of George Bush—and as a private observer, was also kind enough to contribute the foreword to this publication.

I am grateful to the five persons whose names appear on the back cover who graciously wrote words of encouragement to prospective readers. I value their recommendations because each of them played a major role in the negotiation of NAFTA, the public and congressional debate leading to its adoption, or both. They are Carla Hills, the U.S. Trade Representative during the most active phase of the negotiations; Robert Mosbacher, who, as secretary of commerce, traveled extensively in Mexico and the United States explaining the benefits of the agreement as he saw them; Ann Richards, the former governor of Texas, the state with the greatest commercial relationship with Mexico; William Richardson of New Mexico, now the U.S. ambassador to the United Nations, who played a major role in the House of Representatives in the NAFTA debate; and Peter Hakim, president of the Inter-American Dialogue, an institution that lives up to its name of encouraging dialogue on hemispheric issues.

I wish to thank John Melle, director of the Mexico program in the Office of the U.S. Trade Representative, for specific help on the operations of NAFTA. Two analysts from the U.S. Department of Commerce, Douglas Karmin and Helene Stevens, provided much information on trade disputes that have arisen between Mexico and the United States since NAFTA came into effect. I wish to emphasize the help I received from the economic analysis staff of the U.S. International Trade Commission. This was done at a number of meetings organized by Robert A. Rogowsky, director of operations, and through written material of the ITC staff. My judgment is that the most unbiased and comprehensive official material published on NAFTA is done by the research staff of the ITC because its independent position in the U.S. governmental structure encourages professional analysis rather than pre-cooked positions.

The Mexico program of CSIS, represented by Delal Baer and Armand Peschard-Sverdrup, provided the encouragement and financing for this publication. James O'Brien, then an intern at CSIS, gathered many of the documents that provided the raw material for the discussion in the publication. Carolyn Blackwell, my assistant, is responsible for getting the manuscript in shape and preparing the graphs in chapter 3. This is a much improved product over the original manuscript because of the dedicated editorial help from Roberta Howard of the CSIS publications office.

The material and opinions in this monograph are mine and not those of CSIS as an institution, and not necessarily those of any of the people who provided help and commentary.

SIDNEY WEINTRAUB
Washington, D.C.
February 1997

1

Introduction

Many U.S. government agencies periodically assess the progress of the North American Free Trade Agreement. They do this because of their mandates, coupled with pressure from the U.S. Congress. The Department of Commerce does this for overall NAFTA trade and for interchange in specific sectors. The Department of Agriculture's NAFTA economic monitoring task force makes periodic reports and was up to NAFTA-6 at the end of 1996. Regular reports come from the International Trade Commission, the Office of the U.S. Trade Representative, the State Department, the Labor Department, the Environmental Protection Agency—to name just some of the reporting agencies. There is now an elaborate network of intragovernmental committees. The Congressional Research Service of the Library of Congress issues a steady stream of analyses for the Congress, and the General Accounting Office has provided a number of oversight assessments. Most of the output is in hard copy and generally available electronically.

The facts presented in the executive agency reports tend to be impeccably correct, but they have a pro-NAFTA bias. The administration of Bill Clinton, after all, supports NAFTA—although this was hard to tell during the 1996 electoral season. So, too, did the administration of George Bush, but this also was hard to fathom from the Republican Party electoral rhetoric in 1996.

There is also a constant drumbeat of anti-NAFTA discourse emanating from established anti-NAFTA groups. These include the AFL-CIO, organizations established under the aegis of Ralph Nader, unreconciled environmental organizations, left-leaning think tanks complemented in this task by the ultranationalist right wing of the Republican Party, and, of course, Ross Perot and his supporters. Most of this material is not just anti-NAFTA, but against free (or, if one prefers another word, open) trade.

1

Most of the material with which the public is bombarded is therefore one-sided advocacy. Just about all of it is partial. The automobile producers love NAFTA, the unions in this industry despise it, and their respective press releases and publications reflect these positions. Groups that have always opposed NAFTA tell us that the Mexican side of the border is just as polluted, maybe even more so, as when NAFTA went into effect on January 1, 1994;[1] at the same time, those who have always supported NAFTA inform us about all the institutions that did not exist before that are now working on border environmental problems.

Newspapers and television talk shows, in their zeal to demonstrate impartiality, carry op-ed columns and talking heads from the extremes—rabidly anti-NAFTA (and anti-imports from just about anywhere) partisans arguing with those who see no fault in the way NAFTA is functioning. The "silent majority," those who see merit in the NAFTA concept but who are also critical of some features of the agreement, is less well represented.

It is not surprising, therefore, that the public that truly wishes information about the agreement is pretty well fed up with discussions of NAFTA. Non-experts and those not directly involved in the economic interchange with Mexico—those not competing with imports from Mexico and not profiting from exports to Mexico—have not been well informed about how the agreement is working. Instead, they are subjected to sound bites and isolated anecdotes generalized as inevitable verities. The purpose of this progress report is to fill in some of the gaps in the information regularly distributed to the public.

Fair-minded analysts—those who support the idea of greater economic integration between the United States and its two land neighbors, as I do, and those who oppose it—must admit that it is too early to make any definitive judgment about NAFTA's effects.[2] Why then am I writing now? I do this with diffidence because it will take time, ten years or more, before we know how the countries have adapted and restructured their economies to their growing economic integration. Mexico suffered the most severe economic decline in any year of its modern history in 1995 and this has overwhelmed all other short-term effects, including those of NAFTA.

My purpose is to put NAFTA into its proper context. The views of financially interested parties are largely caricatures. So are many of the one-sided government studies written by persons who are not free agents. NAFTA cannot be assessed by looking at one year's trade data, as both supporters and opponents do. NAFTA, in this view, was good for the United States in 1994 because the country had a bilateral trade surplus with Mexico, but bad in 1995 when the surplus turned into a deficit. Crass mercantilism of this nature should have gone out of fashion with Adam Smith some 220 years ago.

Even more sharply, assessing the effects of the agreement by looking at annual and even monthly trade balances—which side is ahead because its bilateral exports of the moment exceed its imports—borders on deception. Temporary trade balance measurements between two countries in a global trading system tell us very little. Honest commercial interchange is not between winners and losers. Who gets the better of the deal, the realtors who have money inflow when they sell homes, or the home buyers who must lay out money? Who's ahead, the grocer or the shopper? Whose welfare should we measure when Mexican tomatoes capture a larger share of the U.S. market—the Florida growers or the U.S. consumers?

While NAFTA is an agreement among three countries, what follows will focus on the U.S.-Mexico situation. The Canada-U.S. trade relationship has its specific conflicts, sometimes quite bitter, but the overall situation is not basically contentious.[3] The Canada-U.S. Free Trade Agreement, which went into effect in 1989, sailed through the congressional approval process with little discussion and even less controversy. By contrast, what was probably the most contentious national and congressional trade debate since the Smoot-Hawley tariff measures of 1930 erupted over free trade with Mexico. Trade integration with Mexico represented something new because of Mexico's status as a developing country and one right on the U.S. border. The agreement with Canada was also groundbreaking for U.S. trade policy, but was traditional at its core because Canada is a highly developed economy.

What follows will try to be reasonably comprehensive—without being prolix or too technical about the agreement's provisions or too theoretical in the economic analysis—in assessing the operation of NAFTA thus far. It would have been preferable to wait a number of years before reaching conclusions about NAFTA, but the political contention over the agreement precludes endless patience.

This progress report begins by setting forth the criteria by which an economic integration agreement of this nature should be assessed. The economic-political-social situation in Mexico will be described because this is necessary to understanding the functioning of the agreement. The bulk of the discussion will deal with developments in specific fields—trade, investment, finance, and the development of internal and cooperative institutions spawned by the combination of the internal situation in Mexico and the requirements of NAFTA.

2

How to Evaluate NAFTA

The most important disservice inflicted on NAFTA by its supporters in the Clinton administration was to base the campaign for congressional approval on unadulterated mercantilism. Administration spokesmen again and again stressed that NAFTA would increase the U.S. merchandise trade surplus with Mexico. This stance was not unique to the Clinton years; those responsible for building support for NAFTA in the Bush administration did the same. The emphasis is understandable in political terms; this is what the Congress wanted to hear and what media commentary stressed.

During both administrations, export expansion was equated with job creation. The most common equation was that each additional $1 billion of exports creates 20,000 U.S. jobs. Thus, when U.S. merchandise exports to Mexico increased by more than $9 billion during 1994, the first year of the agreement, this was touted as creating 180,000 jobs. By the same token, when U.S. merchandise exports to Mexico declined by $5 billion in 1995, the agreement's opponents took up the drumbeat and argued that U.S. employment during this second year of NAFTA fell by 100,000, even though it is most inexact to treat the employment consequences of imports in precisely the same manner as for increased exports. What's sauce for the goose is not always sauce for the gander.

Just about all the arguments about the trade balance and job loss and creation in the previous paragraph are 95 percent rubbish. A bilateral merchandise trade balance, particularly one that is changing year to year, is not a significant measurement. There is no automatic relationship between increased export value and job creation, and certainly not between increased imports and job losses. The figure of 20,000 jobs gained for each $1 billion of exports used by the Department of Commerce, and then repeated endlessly, comes from primitive arithmetic and is wrong. A report of the Congressional Research Service (CRS) notes that the arithmetic for 1995 comes closer to 14,000 jobs for $1 billion of exports, and neither should this be taken seriously.[1]

Merchandise trade is only one element of the U.S. balance of payments. The current account of the balance of payments also includes trade in services, which is about 20 percent the value of merchandise trade. Even more significantly, it is impossible to separate merchandise from service trade. For example, the United States imports VCRs but more than compensates by its booming exports of videos, which are many times more important. Shouldn't the two at least be discussed together? When the computer is used to facilitate manufacturing, is the resulting export a good or a service? Clearly, it is a combination of both and none of our trade data captures this amalgam.

The following discussion first examines the wrong criteria for assessing the results of NAFTA. These, unfortunately, dominate the political and media attention. This will be followed by a discussion of the more salient criteria that should be used. This analysis will make clear why three years of existence is insufficient for measuring the basic structural changes set in motion when countries seek to integrate their economies.

Earlier, the rubbish content of the arguments that now dominate the public debate on NAFTA was placed at 95 percent. The reason for the remaining 5 percent is that there is some truth to the position that exports and imports affect jobs, that trade between Mexico and the United States has grown since NAFTA came into existence and this increase may have been one effect of NAFTA (*may* have been, because it is hard to establish cause and effect), and that balance-of-payments positions of countries can matter. But these phenomena can be analyzed only when dealt with in more sophisticated fashion than bumper-sticker slogans.

Balance-of-Payments Accounting

For the reader not familiar with balance-of-payments accounting and terminology, a simplified description may be useful in order to follow the arguments that are presented.

Balance-of-payments statistics seek to measure a country's transactions with the rest of the world. The data are most frequently shown by calendar years, but information is released more frequently, such as on a monthly basis for merchandise trade. Various accounting conventions exist, which change over time, about how best to present the balance-of-payments data for accuracy and as a tool of analysis. In broad terms, there are three separate measurements in a balance-of-payments presentation: the current account; the capital account; and then, to make the double-entry bookkeeping balance at the end, an item showing the change in reserves.

The *current account* measures those transactions that took place in the period presented and includes merchandise trade, trade in services, payment of interest on debt, and various similar transactions. The measure is designed to give a picture of whether the country is currently earning enough to meet its immediate expenditures. If the current account is in deficit—if more is being spent than is earned—this must be financed in some fashion. This can be compared with a household that can spend more than its current income *only* if it goes into debt or has savings on which to draw.

The same is true for a country. This is an important point to remember for the Mexican situation in 1995. In that year, portfolio capital—foreign currency equity and debt investment—into Mexico more or less ceased and Mexico had run out of foreign reserves. Mexico, in other words, could not borrow very much abroad and had no savings (reserves) on which to draw. The country therefore had to live within its immediate means and could do this only if its current account deficit were eliminated or sharply reduced. Under these circumstances, imports of goods and services had to decline, or exports had to rise, or some combination of the two.

The financing is shown in the *capital account*, which measures investments and debt transactions. The capital account is said to be in surplus if more capital is coming in than is leaving the country. Omitting the change in reserves for the moment, it is thus evident in this way of keeping accounts that a country must have a capital account surplus if it is to finance a current account deficit: more capital must come in if more is being spent on a current basis than is being earned. The two accounts therefore normally have opposite signs, and a current account deficit signifies a capital account surplus.

Traditionally, it was expected that a developing country should run a modest current account deficit and finance its current development needs by drawing on foreign capital, or, to use another term, foreign savings. This was the typical Mexican situation before the hurly-burly 1980s and the years of debt crisis.

Countries typically try to build *foreign reserves*, the third major section of the balance-of-payments accounts, so that temporary current account deficits that are not counterbalanced by capital inflows can be handled without a crisis. This is the element that is compared above with a family building up its savings for a rainy day.

In December 1994, Mexico was practically out of reserves at the same time that its current account deficit was skyrocketing. Mexico had few options at that point, all bad: to put restrictions on imports because the funds to pay for them did not exist; to put controls on capital outflows in order to guard the reserves that did exist; or to devalue the currency, which, by changing relative prices between tradeable and non-tradeable goods, could stimulate exports and impede imports and therefore alter the current account balance. It was just such a choice, what amounted to an attempted devaluation of up to 15 percent on December 20, that led to a run on the peso and transformed a crisis into a disaster. The disaster might have been worse and longer-lasting had either of the other two options been chosen. The existence of NAFTA actually limited Mexico's choices because either import restrictions or exchange controls would have destroyed the agreement.

The merchandise trade picture normally is the main part of the current account. But because it is only part of the total picture, and variable at that, the technicians who compile the accounts and the experts who analyze them are in constant despair about media highlighting of monthly and even annual merchandise trade figures. The technicians try to obscure somewhat the deficit or surplus aspect by showing this in a memorandum item and not in the main body of the presentation. It has been a losing game. The media invariably emphasize the horse-race aspect of the balance of payments—the performance of the merchandise trade picture, whether it is improving (a bigger surplus or a smaller deficit) or deteriorating. For a country like Mexico, a larger trade deficit (deterioration in the horse-race metaphor) may be just what is necessary in normal times. But 1995 and 1996 were not normal. Mexico was in no position in those years to sustain a trade deficit, let alone a current account deficit of any magnitude.

Incorrect Criteria for Evaluating NAFTA

These will be discussed separately, even though they are conceptually linked.

1. The Merchandise Trade Balance

Two points should be kept in mind when looking at the U.S.-Mexican bilateral merchandise trade balance:

- The United States is a world trader and any specific bilateral balance has little relevance for the global U.S. trade picture. A rational analysis of trade performance would start with the premise that the United States should have a trade deficit with some countries and a surplus with others, depending on how each country's tastes, resources, and economic structure mesh with our own.

- The relative macroeconomic positions of two trading partners will have a determining effect on their bilateral balance.[2] A country whose economy is robust will suck in imports and one that is in decline will not. Put differently, one should expect shifts in the bilateral trade balance.

The U.S. government put much emphasis on the U.S. merchandise trade surplus with Mexico when NAFTA was being debated; the U.S. surplus that year, 1993, was $1.7 billion, positive but modest. The argument was that the surplus would most likely increase as Mexico hit its development stride and its import demands burgeoned. The U.S. surplus declined marginally to $1.3 billion in 1994, but it was still positive. By then, however, the tenor of the trade argument began to change and the emphasis shifted to the large increase in U.S. exports to Mexico as a result of NAFTA as opposed to the balance between exports and imports. There was no rigorous effort to relate cause (NAFTA) and effect (U.S. exports), other than to assert that the export increase could be explained by the increased margin of preference for U.S. goods as Mexico reduced its tariffs only for its free-trade partners. By 1995, the pro-NAFTA rationale in official documents was that despite the decline in U.S. exports to Mexico that year, they were still higher than they had been in 1993, before NAFTA.[3] The trade data were subjected to typical political spin.

On the whole, however, the trade arguments in favor of NAFTA in official government documents began to take on a more economically defensible tone as the reality of what was happening was absorbed. What started as a bilateral trade-surplus basis for supporting NAFTA shifted to a trade-increase explanation. The Department of Commerce has a penchant for praising U.S. export increases rather than growth in two-way trade, but the latter is at least shown in the analyses.

Material from the AFL-CIO highlights the shift in the U.S.-Mexican merchandise trade balance from a steadily declining U.S. surplus from 1992 through 1994 to the large, $15 billion U.S. deficit in 1995.[4] If the bilateral trade data are taken back even further, however, say, to 1987 as Mexico began to recover modestly from its economic crisis of 1982, what they show is the declining U.S. merchandise trade *deficit* with Mexico that moved into surplus for the United States only in 1991. The bilateral trade data of the last decade support the position that it is less the trade policy of the moment that determines annual bilateral trade balances but, rather, the macroeconomic conditions in the two countries.

The rejection of shifting annual bilateral trade balances between the United States and Mexico as a valid criterion for assessing NAFTA is not intended to deny that Mexico is an important market. It is, in fact, the third largest destination for U.S. merchandise exports, after Canada and Japan. The Mexican market is even more lucrative in terms of U.S. value added than the Japanese market. In the way the U.S. Census Bureau calculates these things, manufactured exports to Mexico in 1994 were $44 billion, and only $35 billion to Japan.

Exports matter, and they do create jobs. But even on these measures, the Mexico relationship is a minor factor in the health of the U.S. economy. This point can be brought home with some simple data. In 1994, the "successful" year for NAFTA because there was a bilateral U.S. merchandise trade surplus, Mexico took 10 percent of U.S. worldwide exports. Global merchandise exports that year represented about 7.5 percent of U.S. gross domestic product (GDP). Total exports to Mexico therefore amounted to 0.75 percent of U.S. GDP (one-tenth of 7.5 percent). If just the increase in exports to Mexico in that good year is the yardstick, then this represented about one-tenth of 1 percent of U.S. GDP.

When one uses the trade-balance measure, the unstated calculation is that exports are good and imports are bad. One must ask why so many people believe this is so. Why did the U.S. government push the trade-balance argument when seeking approval of NAFTA and why do the AFL-CIO and others continue to do this? The answer is not self-evident.

One reason may be a neo-mercantilist sense of prestige and economic independence, based on the belief that a country that sells more than it buys on a current basis does not have to depend on foreign savings to finance its current account deficit. To the extent that this sentiment has any validity at all—and it is hard to see that it does for the United States except in nationalistic terms—this must be related to a global balance, not to any particular bilateral balance.

If the United States were able to convert a global current account deficit into a surplus, what would be done with the accumulation?[5] Accumulating more gold, as the mercantilists wished, no longer has any resonance. These resources could be used, however, to provide more foreign aid, reduce the external debt of the United States, or be added to reserves. Those who focus on the trade and current account position rarely have much to say about this. It is not generally a relevant issue for them.

The trade-balance emphasis does flow logically into protectionism. Many euphemisms are used to camouflage this; the desire is for "fair," not free, trade; not for protectionism, but for a "level playing field." In the final analysis, however, the political rationale of the trade-balance argument translates into the jobs issue. It seems almost not to matter to those who focus on the trade-balance issue what it costs to keep jobs at home in protected industries. Hufbauer and Elliott estimated that it cost consumers an average of $170,000 a year, based on the level of protection that existed in 1990, for each job that was saved in 21 sectors they examined, or, as they put it, "over six times the average annual compensation of manufacturing workers to preserve jobs through import restraints."[6] At any rate, one must ask whether job and wage preservation and augmentation are valid criteria for assessing NAFTA.

2. Jobs and Wages

As with the modest role that trade with Mexico has on the U.S. economy, one must keep in perspective the potential job loss and creation for the U.S. economy brought into play by NAFTA.

In the years since NAFTA came into existence the U.S. economy has been generating about 2.25 million jobs a year. For the first six months of 1996, nonfarm payrolls added 1.3 million workers, slightly better than the 1.2 million payroll addition during the first half of 1995.[7] Unemployment in the United States, while it varies month to month, averaged around 5.5 percent in 1996. There has been no overall lack of job creation during the years since NAFTA came into effect.

There is a program of trade adjustment assistance administered by the U.S. Department of Labor to provide help for workers who lose their jobs because of import competition from Mexico and Canada or because production moves from the United States to those two countries. As of mid-1996, that is, after two and one-half years of NAFTA's existence, 78,038 workers were certified under the program as having lost their jobs. These certifications amounted to fewer jobs than were created every 10 working days in the United States during those 30 months.

The AFL-CIO doubts that these certifications capture all displaced workers, either because of lack of knowledge of the program, lack of eligibility for workers in service industries like truck driving, or the cumbersome nature of the program. The figures, on the other hand, may be overstated because certification can be obtained by relating production movement to imports from Mexico or Canada without necessarily showing that the imports were caused by the NAFTA agreement.

The adjustment assistance program, despite its defects, does provide a basis for some measurement of job losses due to increased import competition. The U.S. government does not have any comparable way to measure job gains from NAFTA. This is why primitive measuring formulas, like 20,000 jobs to $1 billion of exports, are bandied about. This failure of reciprocal measurement is hardly crucial, however, because the role of trade with Mexico in either job creation or job loss in the United States is marginal.

Even if understated by a factor of two or three, job losses due to NAFTA are dwarfed by other developments in the U.S. economy. The same would be true for job gains as a result of NAFTA, if we tried to measure these. This is the main reason why job measurement is a faulty criterion for evaluating NAFTA. Job creation and loss are overwhelmingly a function of conditions in the U.S. economy. Foreign trade with a single country is marginal in this respect. Macroeconomic policy—monetary policy of the Federal Reserve Board, the management of fiscal policy, and shifts in the value of dollar in relation to other currencies—is much more significant than trade outcomes, particularly with a single country like Mexico, in determining domestic employment.

The major concern of the Fed during the period that NAFTA has been in effect is that unemployment is approaching what is often referred to as the natural rate or, its near relative, the nonaccelerating inflation rate of unemployment (NAIRU), that is, the unemployment rate that is consistent with keeping inflation from rising. The Fed may or may not have acted correctly, but act it did in 1994 by raising short-term interest rates to slow down the rate of GDP growth because of this concern about inflation. The Fed, in other words, deliberately tried to limit U.S. job growth. The U.S. stock and bond markets plummeted after the record increase in payroll additions in June 1996 raised fears of renewed inflation. The concern was that too many jobs were being created and that this could not be sustained.

The dominant national concern of the authorities in the United States since NAFTA has been in existence, therefore, is that the United States has been creating too many jobs. This fear certainly does not reflect any general concern over job loss at a national level because of NAFTA. The fear of insufficient job creation in the United States will surely recur when the economy slows down or moves into recession, but the corrective medicine will focus on macroeconomic policy, not on trade with Mexico.

Much the same is true for what has been called "runaway" investment to take advantage of cheap labor in Mexico, U.S. presidential candidate Ross Perot's "sucking sound." Direct U.S. investment in plant and equipment in Mexico in 1994 was $3 billion, or about one-third of 1 percent of U.S. gross private domestic investment of more than $1 trillion that year. The foreign direct investment (FDI) that goes to Mexico from the United States is largely lost in the "noise" that accompanies the effort to measure the investment that takes place at home.

The effect on jobs of imports and shifting production from one location to another does raise a real human issue in particular sectors and localities. Even 78,000 job losses, the number certified over two and one-half years, creates real hardships for the people affected, their families, and potentially their communities. But this is a different sort of issue from the total effect on jobs in the United States as a result of NAFTA. Keeping out foreign or Mexican goods is an expensive way to deal with the job-loss problems that do not affect the entire economy.

Imports and exports are not completely separable transactions, contrary to the position of those who would limit imports to conserve U.S. jobs. This point will be developed more fully later when examining what should be the valid criteria for evaluating the success or failure of NAFTA. An import restraint may translate into an export limitation due to the inability of the exporting country to earn the dollars to buy U.S. products. Those who deplore the joint production of goods under which parts of final products are made in a number of foreign locations seem to conclude that if this practice were halted, then the entire production would take place in the United States. This is the implicit assumption of those who criticize the *maquiladora* system, which uses precisely this coproduction for further processing of U.S. inputs using Mexican labor. It is even more likely, however, that if coproduction were halted, the entire production would move out of the United States.

Nor are exports and imports reciprocal in their job effects. Additional exports may or may not increase employment, depending on whether they represent an increase in production that would not otherwise have taken place domestically. These extra exports might result from a shift in marketing from within the country to a foreign country because of exchange-rate advantages or some type of export subsidy. They may come about due to higher productivity, that is, higher output by the same number of workers. The probability is high, however, that increased exports, if sustained, will translate over time into more jobs, even if only at the margin, or into higher wages as productivity rises.

Increased imports may or may not lead to job losses. They will—at least for a particular plant or company or industry, even if not necessarily for the economy as a whole—if they replace domestic production. They need not have any adverse job effect if they are inputs that otherwise are not available and are incorporated into domestic products. U.S. fuel imports from Mexico in 1995 were $5.8 billion and these surely had no adverse job impact. If Fed policy is designed to keep unemployment at the natural rate, that is, to prevent excessive job increases, this implies that the issue of job losses from extra imports is not germane. At such times—which in fact have prevailed since NAFTA has been in existence—the additional imports represent the availability of more goods and services than would otherwise be the case. As long as output and employment continue to rise, "[n]ew imports are just *added* to domestic output and not *substituted* for it."[8]

A word on wage effects of NAFTA: This is potentially a more relevant issue for evaluating NAFTA than job losses, although there is no hard or precisely quantified evidence to date that U.S. wages have suffered from the agreement. The danger is that U.S. plants in which wage costs are an important element of total costs will close in order to open somewhere else where wage rates are lower. Mexico offers one such possibility. NAFTA augments Mexico's attraction because of the preferential treatment imports from there receive in the U.S. market. The Mexican tariff advantage over other low-wage countries should not be exaggerated because a large proportion of Mexican products enjoyed duty-free entry into the United States before NAFTA under the U.S. general system of preferences. In addition, maquiladora output paid the U.S. duty only on the value added outside the United States, so that the extra tariff preference from NAFTA is modest. Finally, U.S. duties are low, which means that margins of preference are not normally great.

The workers most at risk are in industries that depend on low wages for their viability. The industry most often cited is textile products, for which data will be provided in the next chapter. As this was written a safeguard investigation was under way by the International Trade Commission to determine if increased imports of what are referred to as broom-corn brooms since NAFTA were causing or threatening to cause serious injury to the competitive U.S. industry;[9] and, in the end, import restrictions were imposed. This is a stereotypical low-wage industry for which import relief has been sought for decades, that is, since long before NAFTA. The consequences of increased imports are important to those who work to make competitive brooms, but not to the country at large.

Two opposing points can be made about imports competing with low-wage domestic production. On one hand, the workers in these industries are the most vulnerable in the United States and may have no alternative if they lose their jobs. Their wages cannot go much lower than they are now. For these reasons, they may need help from the government. On the other hand, there is no future for the United States as a country to compete with Mexico or other developing countries on the basis of paying low wages. These two contradictory considerations make this a hard issue to deal with.

Relevant Criteria for Evaluating NAFTA

NAFTA is a trade agreement and, therefore, the effect it has on trade flows is a relevant measure of the agreement's success. It is also an agreement that encourages investment in the member countries, particularly for plant and equipment, and the extent and nature of this investment are highly germane. Above all, the purpose of NAFTA is to facilitate economic integration in North America—that is, to encourage thinking in terms of one large regional economic area rather than three separate ones—and the crux of any evaluation must assess whether this objective is being achieved. Finally, the facilitation of these objectives requires changes in institutions to facilitate cooperation among the member countries of NAFTA and procedures for the expeditious resolution of conflicts.

The details in each of these areas will be provided in subsequent chapters. What follows here is an explanation of why these are the relevant variables for evaluating NAFTA.

1. Increase in Total Trade

If trade is viewed as a positive-sum venture, what matters is whether all the parties to trade transactions benefit. If they do not, the trade surely will cease—why trade if the outcome is deleterious? The NAFTA issue as it relates to the United States and Mexico, therefore, is not the bilateral trade balance between them, but whether the total trade increase that derives from NAFTA is mutually beneficial. Are the exports (and imports) of both parties increasing? Is total trade going up?

There is a constraint in using this measure, namely, whether the trade increase between members of an integration arrangement takes place at the expense of nonmember, or third, countries. This is referred to in the literature as the trade-creation as opposed to the trade-diversion effect.[10] Trade creation results from the tariff reductions between member countries inherent in an integration agreement, and trade diversion from the shifting of trade from what before was the most competitive exporting country in favor of the integration partner who now enjoys a preferential advantage. This trade creation/trade diversion aspect is the reason why the General Agreement on Tariffs and Trade (GATT) and, now, the World Trade Organization (WTO) require that the tariffs after an integration arrangement be no higher than before.

Latin American and Caribbean countries entered into a number of integration agreements in the 1960s and 1970s. That was when those countries still sought industrial development through import substitution; that is, they employed high tariffs and other import barriers to protect what they considered to be infant industries. In those circumstances, economic integration was seen as a way of enlarging the market while still practicing import substitution. Tariffs and other border barriers were high against nonmembers. The result was not only damaging trade diversion, but also highly unbalanced benefits in favor of the more competitive countries within the protected bloc. As a result, all the agreements collapsed or were reshaped. The current model in the region is "open regionalism," that is, integration behind low barriers, with membership open to all those regional countries seeking to join.[11] Unfortunately, some of the tariffs in Latin America are too high to allow their regional agreements to be called "open"—Brazil's tariffs for automobiles, for example.

The NAFTA countries have low barriers. The average post–Uruguay Round most-favored-nation (MFN) nonagricultural tariff level, that which applies to products from countries with which they do not have free-trade agreements, will be 3 percent for the United States and about 10 percent for Mexico. On the whole, this should limit trade diversion, although not necessarily for all products. Trade diversion may have been substantial, for example, for exports of Mexican textile products to the United States because of NAFTA provisions combined with the global import-quota regime (the Multifiber Arrangement) that still exists in this sector. NAFTA's rule of origin in the automotive sector also lends itself to trade diversion.

As will be shown in the next chapter, total U.S.-Mexican trade has increased for both countries since NAFTA went into effect, although the results are distorted by the sharp decline in Mexico's GDP in 1995. There may also have been some trade diversion in 1995 in that the decline in Mexico's imports was less for U.S. products than for those from other regions.

2. Intra-Industry Trade and Specialization

Non-economists, including politicians, tend to think that integration between countries is desirable when the countries have complementary production. If country A produces largely agricultural products and country B industrial ones, then, so the thinking goes, they can trade with each other without market or employment disruption. Under these circumstances, however, there is no need for economic integration. The trade will take place in any event.

To the economist, integration is most valuable when it allows countries to specialize within the same overall industry or economic sector. In this way, economies of scale can be developed. Foreign economic integration in Western Europe started with the Coal and Steel Community. For the United States and

Canada, it began with the automobile agreement of 1965. There had been some matching of U.S. and Canadian auto duties earlier, but the 1965 pact was a critical step. In both cases, trade within these overall sectors increased many times over the years.

The most important export of each of the three NAFTA countries to one another is in the automotive industry. This results from specialization in plants of optimum size. Some plants focus on smaller cars, others on larger ones; some dominate in the production of engines, others of body parts, and still others of related products.

One must therefore ask how much specialization NAFTA has induced. Phrased another way, has trade within the same industrial sectors—intra-industry trade—increased? Have producers taken advantage of the particular factors that are most favorable for production and marketing in each of the countries such that output can be maximized at the least cost?

We know that is what happens domestically. Michigan and Ohio trade extensively with each other in all varieties of related products. So, too, must Michigan and Ontario if free trade is to work. At the southern border, so too must Texas and Mexico. Both Texas and Mexico produce chemicals and petrochemicals; each produces a variety of agricultural products; each provides such services as trucking and insurance—and the question is how much their mutual trade in these same sectors is growing.

The growth of specialization and of intra-industry trade are not criteria that are readily grasped by non-experts. They imply adaptation to changing production and marketing demands, which in turn involve some dislocation. This happens regularly within countries—textile production moves south, auto production is diversified, and computer software innovation spreads from Silicon Valley to Austin, Texas, and beyond. It must occur across countries if free trade is to be meaningful. The ultimate test is whether all the countries benefit from economic expansion and are able to compensate for the disruption that is inevitable. Maintaining the status quo is not an option. The issue is to confront the dynamics that always are at play.

Thomas L. Friedman, in an op-ed column in the *New York Times*, emphasized the imperative of countries to make the transition from relatively closed societies to the global marketplace.[12] Mexico faced this requirement for adjustment after its economic collapse in 1982. The crux of the debate in Canada on entering into the free-trade agreement with the United States that came into force on January 1, 1989, was over "little" Canada (in an economic sense) or adjustment to the changing global reality.

Much of the international trade of the three NAFTA countries is conducted by multinational corporations (MNCs) that produce and market in all three countries. Up to 60 to 70 percent of this trade is not in final products, but in inputs into these products. As is well known, there is no such thing as an exclusively U.S. automobile; there are cars assembled in the United States from parts produced in scores of countries. Much the same is true for the production of chemicals, pharmaceuticals, electronic products, and textile products.

There is no escape from the globalization that exists, despite America Firsters and politicians playing on ultranationalism. Companies globalize to increase their competitive positions and to obtain access to markets. Countries must embrace globalization or be left behind in the quest for higher incomes. The main purpose of economic integration arrangements is to best exploit these realities. Just as neither Canada nor Mexico could prosper by relying excessively on domestic markets, neither can there be a "little" United States in the modern world economy.

3. Productivity and Wages

The only way to sustain a steady increase in real wages, that is, nominal increases that are not wiped out by inflation, is through increases in productivity, that is, output per worker. Higher productivity does not always translate into immediate wage increases; but without higher productivity, wages will surely stagnate.

Economists are not able to separate out all the elements that lead to productivity increases. Some of the generally accepted explanations for growth in productivity are a more educated work force, improvements in technology, innovation in production techniques, growth in direct investment, less restrictive regulations, and a competitive climate in which less successful firms fall by the wayside rather than be rescued by taxpayer funds. Most of these elements are generated within the domestic economy of a country as developed as the United States. Domestic considerations also are crucial in Mexico, but the basic motivation for the opening of the Mexican economy during the 1980s was to enhance its industrial productivity through more competition (or less protection against imports) and more ample foreign direct investment. NAFTA, seen in this light, was the logical culmination of Mexico's earlier unilateral economic opening.

Because of the small role that imports from or exports to Mexico play in the U.S. economy, and the relatively minor amount of U.S. direct investment in Mexico compared with domestic investment, the contribution of NAFTA to U.S. productivity will be small for the indefinite future—but not nil. NAFTA is much more important as a potential contributor to Mexico's productivity increases—but still less important than domestic economic and social policy, such as improving the nation's educational structure.

To the extent that it can be done, assessing NAFTA's contribution to productivity increases in either Mexico or the United States is an important criterion for measuring the agreement's value. This will not be pursued here, however, because the measurement cannot easily be calculated accurately. This criterion is cited here because NAFTA has made Mexico more conscious than ever of the need to improve its human skills, attract investment, and have its firms be competitive in both home and foreign markets, especially in the United States.

4. Effect on Competitive Position of Industries

Countries enter into economic integration agreements to maximize the competitive position of their industries. The ability to specialize, to take advantage of economies of scale where they exist, to attract foreign direct investment, are all aspects of this objective. Mexico opened its market unilaterally starting in the mid-1980s largely to stimulate greater efficiency among domestic producers by introducing the import competition that was largely lacking in the import-substitution model. The main reason for doing this was to increase the export competitiveness of firms. NAFTA is best seen as part of this process for Mexico.

NAFTA was supported by large U.S. corporations to permit them to base investment decisions on a combination of efficiency considerations, proximity to market, and the ability to specialize in intermediate production for later incorporation into final products without having to overcome the cost of tariffs and other border barriers. The rationale for *regional* integration is that this process of specialization and trade in intermediate products is facilitated by proximity, which reduces transportation and related costs. There are geographic reasons why Canada is the largest U.S. foreign market and Mexico the third. These regional considerations may diminish over time as transportation and communication costs diminish, but proximity is still important.

Large corporations, MNCs, behave quite similarly throughout the world. As Japanese domestic wages increased, many more production processes that required lesser skills, and therefore demanded lower wages, were exported to other countries in Asia. Regionalism plus the ability to trade in intermediate products were both at work. The Europeans have done the same, based on similar considerations. U.S. corporations have been no different, and while their investments have been global, Mexico and Canada represent for them the best combination of the advantage of geography and the ability to specialize in different locations.

If NAFTA did not exist, the processes outlined here would continue—in Mexico and elsewhere—but without all the other accompaniments provided by a formal agreement, such as those embodied in NAFTA.

5. Effects on the Environment

As economic integration theory was formulated over the last half century, environmental issues did not figure in the equation until NAFTA. Trade theorists just did not think about the environmental considerations. GATT, when written, contained some general references to environmental matters, but nothing of consequence. NAFTA, as many commentators have pointed out, brought out the connection between trade and the environment.[13] This linkage is now debated in the WTO, the Organization for Economic Cooperation and Development (OECD), and other international institutions.

The connection between the two subjects is not without controversy. Both Mexico and the United States were drawn kicking and screaming into linking trade and the environment by the pressure from environmental groups. Mexico consented under U.S. pressure, and the basic NAFTA agreement therefore contains a number of important environmental provisions, for example, the incorporation of some important international environmental and conservation agreements. President Clint— later insisted on parallel agreements on environmen cooperation as a condition of U.S. support for NAF the most ardent proponents of free trade, especially ness community and supported by the main body o the Republican Party, oppose the linkage in the parallel agreements. Their argument is that protection of the environment should not be accomplished by potential trade penalties, that new nontariff barriers are thereby created. Many of the most dedicated opponents of free trade, especially in the labor unions and abetted by the main body of opinion in the Democratic Party, ardently promoted the connection. Their argument was that the environment was too important to be omitted. These positions, both for and against the trade-environment linkage, inevitably engender considerable skepticism about true motives.

In any event, NAFTA and the parallel North American Agreement for Environmental Cooperation (NAAEC) do exist. The Commission for Environmental Cooperation (CEC) was established pursuant to the NAAEC. Beyond that, a number of organizations were created to deal with environmental issues along the U.S.-Mexico border, one of the most polluted and environmentally sensitive areas in all of North America.

Whether one likes or dislikes the way the trade-environmental linkage has been incorporated in NAFTA and related agreements, the effectiveness of the environmental effort is a proper subject for evaluation. In this area, however, the limited time the agreement has been in operation is an even more serious impediment to serious evaluation than it is in other areas dealing directly with trade and investment. The same is true for the parallel labor agreement.

Much time was taken in setting up the new environmental bodies, which means that they have not functioned for the full three years NAFTA has been in existence. The powers given to the CEC were limited and it is not clear that the three governments want an aggressive watchdog body. The North American Development Bank (NADBank), designed to help finance environmentally sound infrastructure on the Mexico-U.S. border, must make loans to financially strapped local authorities that often have no means for repayment or funds to make their contributions to the cost of the venture. The Mexican financial contribution for environmental issues was seriously eroded by the economic depression and dire hardships inflicted on the population in 1995 and the incomplete recovery since then.

The evaluation, consequently, must rest more on promise than achievement thus far. The time has been much too brief and the circumstances too unfavorable for substantial accomplishment.[14] The promise is that cooperative environmental bodies have been established, some penalties can be imposed on countries not carrying out their own environmental laws and regulations, and consciousness has been raised about the need for environmental protection. Homegrown environmental nongovernmental organizations (NGOs) have proliferated in Mexico, and this may be the most important development. Environmental protection based on a national desire is certainly more efficacious over the long term than protection imposed from the outside through penalties.

6. Institution Building

Agreements require institutions to make them work. The institutions can be elaborate, like the World Bank, or they can be modest, which is the case for the CEC and its sister organization, the Commission for Labor Cooperation. Institutions are the instruments through which cooperation is carried out.

Perhaps even more important than the institutions themselves are the habits of cooperation that are developed between countries. The authority of institutions is based on what governments wish them to do—and sometimes governments do not wish them to do very much. NAFTA can turn out to be a bust if the member governments take actions that restrict trade in spite of their stated intention to do the opposite or if the benefits are not enjoyed by all the member countries. On the other hand, NAFTA can live up to its promise and turn out to be the most important agreement signed between the United States and Mexico since 1848, when the Treaty of Guadalupe Hidalgo ending the war between the two countries was forced on Mexico.

The Treaty of Guadalupe Hidalgo confirmed U.S. title to Texas and provided for Mexico to cede the huge California and New Mexico territories. Mexico lost half its territory as a result of the war, and this reality has shaped Mexican thinking and the Mexican character ever since. There have been sporadic efforts to smooth out grievances since then, such as the Good Neighbor Policy during the administration of Franklin D. Roosevelt and U.S. financial assistance during various moments of Mexican economic crises, but they lacked the durability to eliminate the deeply held sense of grievance of loss of territory. NAFTA will not change the historical reality either, but it does hold the potential to institutionalize cooperation. A good comparison is the economic union achieved between France and Germany in the European Economic Community, which sought to use economic means to temper the political antagonisms between them.

For Mexico, NAFTA represents an effort to cooperate with the United States, to take advantage of the large market next door, rather than prolong the mistrust that had prevailed. For the United States, NAFTA represents attention to neighborhood that had been largely lacking in the Eurocentric emphasis of U.S. foreign policy. If NAFTA does help bring the economic benefits its supporters posited, this reality can be durable.

The extent and nature of institutional building will be laid out in a later chapter. The key question to ask is whether NAFTA has spawned a new and positive reality in institutional relationships between Mexico and the United States.

The negotiation of NAFTA surely changed the style of Mexico's dealings with the United States, both its executive branch and its legislature. Jorge Montaño, Mexico's ambassador to the United States during the congressional ratification process, has pointed out that Mexican officials ceased dealing almost exclusively with the State Department. The same was true for Gustavo Petrocioli, Mexico's ambassador during the negotiations. Instead, contacts were expanded with all relevant executive agencies and the Congress. Instead of refraining from lobbying activities, which had been earlier practice in the belief that lobbying could be seen as interference with U.S. sovereignty, something that Mexico hoped to prevent in Mexico by the United States, Mexico hired U.S. firms to influence NAFTA ratification. Mexico earlier had looked down on persons of Mexican origin living in the United States, whereas these groups were assiduously cultivated during the NAFTA debate. All these changes persist to this day.

The complex and protracted NAFTA negotiations also brought government officials dealing with substantive matters closer together than had ever been the case previously. This cut across scores of issue areas. These contacts continue today because of the negotiating and consultative working groups set up as a result of NAFTA. The responsible officials from the two countries know each other as never before.[15]

The evaluation must assess the value of these new ways of doing business between U.S. and Mexican officials. It must evaluate the contribution of the new institutional structure that has developed as a consequence of NAFTA.

3

Trade under NAFTA

NAFTA is a free-*trade* agreement and the most direct test of its effectiveness with respect to the United States and Mexico is the extent to which their two-way trade has increased since the agreement went into effect on January 1, 1994. This simple statement needs some nuancing, however.

Trade between the United States and Mexico started to increase before NAFTA came into existence. The causes for this were the recovery in Mexico's economy during the latter years of the 1980s; Mexico's unilateral reduction of import duties starting in 1983 and then accelerating after Mexico joined GATT in 1986 and during the Salinas administration that began in 1988; and the anticipation effect even as NAFTA was under negotiation. Investment in production in Mexico also increased in anticipation of NAFTA, and this increase must be examined in conjunction with the growing trade. It is not sufficient to state that because U.S.-Mexico trade increased after NAFTA, the agreement was therefore the cause of the increase. The *post hoc, ergo propter hoc* fallacy taught to all freshmen in Economics 101 should not be repeated here.[1] The evidence is that NAFTA contributed to the trade increase, but other causations were also at play.

While the key criterion is the increase in two-way trade, it is necessary for there to be some balance in these benefits if the agreement is to endure—not necessarily equivalence in the trade increase, but certainly mutual benefit. What is the composition of the trade increase? Is the theoretical underpinning of economic integration being verified, namely, that the largest trade increases are most likely to result from specialization within industries? Is NAFTA diverting trade away from third countries, or, put differently, are there serious world welfare costs as a result of the increased trade between Mexico and the United States?

Finally, one must ask whether the increase in trade is leading simultaneously to an increase in political pressures for import restrictions. This is hard to measure because, although there is evidence of import protectionism in both countries, there is no reason to believe that this is greater than it would have been without NAFTA, or whether it is more durable. The relevant question, therefore, may be whether the machinery for resolution of trade disputes is superior to what existed before, and here the answer surely is "yes."

U.S.-Mexico Trade

Trade flows between Mexico and the United States will be shown in a number of ways in order to deal with the issues noted above. The intent is to show what has been happening since NAFTA came into existence, but without drowning the reader in excessive detail.

Some general considerations about trade should be kept in mind when interpreting the data that follow. A country's level of imports from all sources depends on a number of considerations. Perhaps the most important is self-evident, namely, that richer countries import more goods and services than do poorer ones. U.S. merchandise exports to Canada in 1995 were $127 billion, whereas those to Mexico were $42 billion. Mexico's population in 1995 was about 91 million and Canada's 29 million. The big difference, however, was in their comparative GDPs, about $250 billion for Mexico and $570 billion for Canada (U.S. dollar equivalents). Put another way, there were $500 of imports from the United States for each Mexican and $4,380 for each Canadian. Total and per capita income is not always a decisive indicator of imports because larger countries, with more diversified production, tend to import less of their GDP than do smaller ones, but it is in this case.

The annual changes in a country's imports are largely a function of changes in GDP. When a country's economy declines, it pulls in less imports; this is part of a self-correcting balance-of-payments adjustment process. Mexico's economy plummeted in 1995 and it was natural for import levels to fall, just as U.S. import levels have been rising in recent years because of the sustained growth in the U.S. GDP.

The share of any country's import market that is captured by different exporting countries has a separate logic. This depends on historical trading links, the familiarity that develops between buyers and sellers, legal frameworks that have been constructed (such as NAFTA), the degree of direct investment and coproduction that exists, and geography. Relative exchange-rate relationships, the cost of export credit, export promotion activities, and the like obviously play a large role. Trade preferences that exist for member countries under NAFTA (and other integration arrangements) obviously affect trade flows; the extent to which this applies depends on the margins of tariff preference and the favoritism under nontariff arrangements, as in the textile product trade that will be discussed later.

Despite improved global transportation and communication links, Canada and Mexico are the number one and number three markets for U.S. exports. Mexico's small GDP, compared with that of many industrial countries, would not normally lead one to expect such a high position for Mexico; nor would its relatively small population lead one to expect Canada to be far and away the largest export market for the United States. Both of these results owe much to the influence of geography and the many relationships encouraged by it over the years, such as the extensive coproduction arrangements between the United States and these two countries.[2] The assurance of predictable treatment established under NAFTA undoubtedly has encouraged increased trade shares for member countries, just as has occurred among the countries of the European Union.

Total Trade Flows

Figure 1 shows the increase in U.S.-Mexico trade starting in 1993, the year before NAFTA went into effect. The two-way trade increase over the three years 1993–1995 was 31.4 percent in nominal dollars, heavily weighted during 1994 before the economic decline in Mexico in 1995. The rate of increase in 1996, based on Department of Commerce data for the first half of the year, continued to be upward of 20 percent; and U.S. exports to Mexico began rising once again as the Mexican economy showed signs of recovery.

One of the consequences of NAFTA is that Mexico was constrained in raising tariffs and other import barriers against U.S. goods because this would have violated the agreement.[3] This turned out to be an important effect of NAFTA. In the past, the instinctive Mexican response to a balance-of-payments crisis was, among other measures, to raise import duties and other border barriers. After 1982, for example, tariffs went up and

Figure 1
U.S.-Mexico Merchandise Trade, 1993–1995
(billions of dollars)

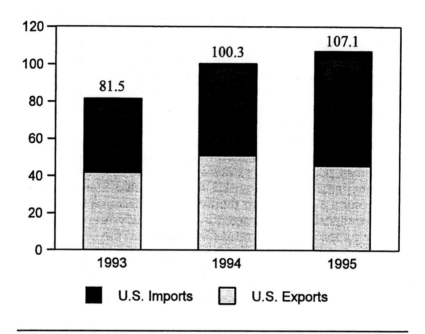

Source: U.S. Department of Commerce.

prior licensing requirements were imposed on 100 percent of Mexico's imports. This time, in 1995, Mexico used macroeconomic measures to deal with the problem. These included a devaluation of the peso (which preceded the economic collapse) and tighter fiscal and monetary policy.

Figure 2 shows that the trade consequences of this way of addressing the balance-of-payments crisis were dramatic. After the 1982 economic downturn, U.S. exports to Mexico declined by 50 percent (as measured from the year before the crisis to the year after). In contrast, after the economic disaster of 1994–1995, U.S. exports measured the same way actually rose by 11 percent. Total U.S.-Mexico trade after 1994 also rose, unlike what happened after 1982.

Make no mistake. What happened during 1995 was a balance-of-payments crisis of immense proportions. Mexico had to correct a current account deficit of some $28 billion, 8 percent of

Figure 2
Change in U.S. Exports to Mexico, 1981–1983 and 1993–1995

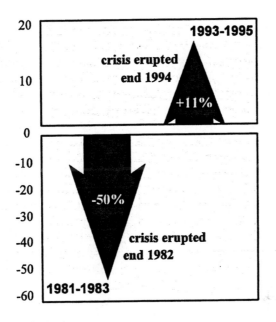

Source: U.S. Department of Commerce.

GDP, in 1995 because portfolio capital ceased entering. Having few international reserves, the country had no way to finance a large current account deficit. The deficit was almost wholly erased in 1995, a huge adjustment. On top of this, there was a GDP decline of almost 7 percent. Domestic demand in Mexico thus fell by 15 percent; a drop of Grand Canyon dimensions. The saving grace for Mexico was that its exports to the United States grew. They might not have had Mexico abandoned its NAFTA commitments because, in that case, the United States almost certainly would have imposed retaliatory import restrictions.

The normal expectation is that mature countries will deal with a balance-of-payments crisis with macroeconomic measures, not import controls. In this sense, Mexico acted like a mature country. The hardships faced by the Mexican population in 1995 and continuing into 1996 were severe. Urban unemployment rose by about one million people and real wages plummeted. But the recovery has been relatively rapid. Mexico started to come out of its 1995 depression by mid-1996, whereas the recovery after 1982 lagged for about five years. Real wages in the years after 1982 fell by about 40 percent, so the gradualism did not shield working men and women.

One can agree or disagree with President Ernesto Zedillo when he told a *Los Angeles Times* interviewer: "Gradualism is not an option, because that would have taken us to total collapse and instead of losing hundreds of thousands of jobs, we would have lost millions. My long-term policy is the best policy in the short term."[4] The choice between gradualism and shock treatment for dealing with an economic crisis of this magnitude has long been argued within the economics profession, and professional opinion is overwhelmingly on Zedillo's side. Politicians, including those in the ruling Partido Revolucionario Institucional (PRI) of Mexico, tend to take the opposite view, that is, to seek to correct the problem more slowly. When translated into deeds, this generally means no correction at all.

One issue in the NAFTA debate was whether the agreement would lock Mexico into an open market, and whether, as a consequence, there would be more predictability in its foreign economic policy. The locking-in hypothesis passed this first test with flying colors.

A powerful case can therefore be made that reliance on macroeconomic measures as opposed to import restrictions was the proper response for Mexico—the proper *economic* response, but one that also had adverse short-term political and social consequences.[5] How did this response affect U.S. trade with Mexico? As figure 2 shows, both U.S. exports to and imports from Mexico fared well as compared with the more gradual economic correction after 1982.

Figure 3 shows this effect on Mexican merchandise imports from the United States compared with Mexican imports from other countries. The data can be interpreted two ways. The first is that the United States, compared with other countries, benefited from the way Mexico handled its balance-of-payments crisis in 1995. U.S. exports to Mexico clearly held up better than those from other sources. The second is less benign, because there surely was some diversion of Mexican import sources in favor of the United States to the detriment of other suppliers. This was a one-year effect in both cases—the relatively favorable trade position of the United States and the adverse consequences for other suppliers—but it does show that preferential trade

Figure 3
Mexico's Imports from Various Sources, 1995
(percentage change from 1994)

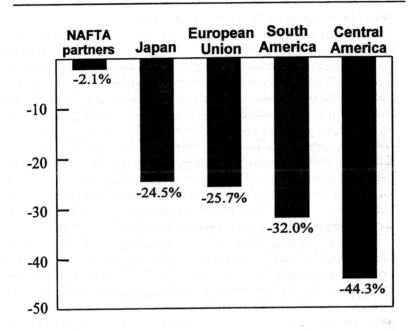

Note: If U.S. data are used, the decline in U.S. exports to Mexico in 1995 was
10.7 percent.
Source: Mexican Embassy, Washington, D.C.

agreements may not augment world welfare. The saving grace is that because the handling of the economic crisis reduced the duration of the income downturn, exports of other countries will pick up again, as they began to do in 1996.

The NAFTA Causation

It would be unwise to single out NAFTA as the only cause of the strong growth in total trade between Mexico and the United States. With the exception of a few years, this two-way trade has grown regularly over the past 20 years. But it is quite startling to note that whereas in 1980 two-way trade was only $28 billion, in 1995 it had grown to $107 billion, and the growth continued in 1996 at double-digit rates from this higher base.

A quarterly trade index constructed at the University of Texas at Austin demonstrates how much this trade has grown since NAFTA went into effect, from 156.76 at the first quarter of 1994 (1990=100) to 200.70 by the second quarter of 1996.[6] A researcher at the Federal Reserve Bank of Dallas attributes much of the increase to NAFTA itself.[7]

In one respect, it is clear that NAFTA was incontrovertibly responsible for the increase in two-way U.S.-Mexico trade. This can be seen if one asks the counterfactual question: What if Mexico had handled its balance-of-payments problems in 1995 the way they were managed in 1983? As Figure 1 shows, total trade increased in 1995, whereas it fell in 1983. The existence of NAFTA explains the different policy conduct.

Putting aside the handling of the 1995 crisis, however, the spectacular two-way trade increase since NAFTA represents the continuation of earlier developments. Trade increased quite consistently once Mexico got past its economic crisis of the 1980s, and particularly after Mexico on its own opened its market to imports and based development on increased exports. Entering into NAFTA, therefore, can be seen as the logical culmination of Mexico's unilateral decisions. NAFTA was a way for Mexico to obtain assurance of an open U.S. market, which had become crucial under its new development policy. In return, Mexico had to provide reciprocal security that its market also would remain open to its NAFTA partners. NAFTA was the instrument for giving legal guaranties to investors and traders of the two countries. The importance of NAFTA is that it provided substantial predictability of treatment for traders and investors.

Foreign direct investment into Mexico had started to rise in anticipation of NAFTA and soared once NAFTA was in effect. From January 1994 through April 1996, FDI totaled $16.5 billion. Even in 1995, the worst year for the Mexican economy since the Great Depression (and perhaps since the Revolution and subsequent civil war), FDI rose by $5.5 billion. Between 1989 and 1994, however, FDI had averaged about $4.5 billion a year.[8] Cumulative FDI in Mexico now exceeds $50 billion, about 62 percent from the United States. (The figures are obtained from cumulative flows and therefore do not necessarily represent actual market value.)

As will be shown in the next section, trade increasingly is between related parties, the result of coproduction arrangements and strategic alliances of various types. These phenomena began before NAFTA went into effect, but have burgeoned now that assurances on the rules of the game are embodied in a legal agreement. Would these forms of trade have grown as much without NAFTA? Possibly, but not likely.

Its proponents give NAFTA almost exclusive credit for the increases in investment between the two countries. The evidence is that NAFTA deserves much credit, as with trade, but some investment growth probably would have occurred in any event. This argument cuts both ways in that the opponents of NAFTA give too much weight to the agreement for stimulating U.S. investment there. NAFTA surely contributed to the investment growth by giving legal form to Mexican assurances of fair treatment, but the investment started to rise once Mexico came out of its slowdown in the 1980s and resumed some degree of economic growth.

Given the nature of the growing economic relations between the two countries, trade and investment must be examined together as part of the same process. Critics of NAFTA often assert that it is an investment and not a trade agreement. The argument is inane; it is both.

In a practical sense, it does not really matter whether NAFTA originated, caused, stimulated, or reinforced the substantial increase in trade and investment between Mexico and the United States. Both have grown. Vested interests have developed on both sides of the border for the continuation of trade growth. It would matter, therefore, if NAFTA were terminated because this would send the unmistakable message of protectionism. Locking out imports from Mexico would surely result in locking out an equivalent amount of U.S. exports to Mexico. Mexico has become too important to too many people in the two countries to return smoothly to the status quo ante (i.e., before NAFTA).

This point became evident during the campaign for the Republican nomination for president. Bob Dole had been struggling against Pat Buchanan before he decisively won the primary in South Carolina "reestablishing himself as the front-runner for the Republican nomination."[9] Buchanan had stressed protection against imports in his campaign, but exit polls in South Carolina showed that fewer than one voter in 10 cited trade as the most important issue affecting their vote. These were the Buchanan supporters. But Buchanan had not fully done his homework because many South Carolina workers were benefiting from NAFTA. South Carolina's exports to Mexico rose by 65 percent in

1994 over 1993, and then rose again by 5.4 percent in 1995, despite the overall decline in U.S. exports to Mexico that year.[10] South Carolina had a vested interest in NAFTA's continuation.

The Specialization Effect

The theoretical underpinning of economic integration is that the elimination of trade and investment barriers will facilitate specialization of production of goods and services. Two countries do not have to integrate their economies if each produces goods not made in the other country. The United States will import coffee regardless of economic integration with, say, Brazil or Colombia. Mexico will purchase large jet aircraft for passenger travel with or without free trade agreements with the countries that manufacture them. The importance of free trade among the 50 U.S. states is not that Kansas can sell wheat and California wines without internal trade barriers, but rather that Michigan and Ohio can specialize in different aspects of the automotive industry and Connecticut and Missouri in the insurance field. Economic integration between countries extends this ability to specialize one degree further, across national boundaries.

Specialization—the division of labor—was analyzed long ago by Adam Smith, using the production of pins as his example. He chose a simple item. Specialization now deals with more complex commodities and services. The international division of labor is a common expression today. The reason for emphasizing specialization is that it facilitates efficient production and, hence, competitiveness. Such labor-intensive tasks as entering data for the on-line reservation systems that make airline travel so seemingly simple to arrange can be done in locations where labor to do this can be obtained at a modest cost. The software for this is produced in the United States and other developed countries. The airplanes are produced in the industrial countries. The connections can be extended much further.

Intra-industry trade. One way to determine whether this specialization is taking place under NAFTA is to examine the nature of production and trade that has developed. Has trade grown most within rather than across industries? The answer is yes.

Two of the 20 leading commodities exported by the United States to Mexico in 1995 were auto parts and internal combustion piston engines. Four of the 20 leading U.S. imports from

Mexico were in the automotive sector, and two of these were parts and engines. The parts and engines that are both imported and exported have identical three-digit SITC numbers, but are differentiated when more detail is added to the description.[11]

The top 20 U.S. imports from and exports to Mexico also include the following, *all in both directions*: electrical machinery; electricity distribution equipment; telecommunications equipment; office machinery parts; furniture; and automatic data processing machinery. Crude oil was the second leading U.S. import from Mexico, and oil products the fifteenth most important U.S. export to Mexico. The number of comparable products shipped in both directions remains extensive when one gets beyond the top 20. They include plastics and plastic products, iron and steel, fertilizers, sulfur, and wood products. The United States ships fabrics to Mexico and Mexico has become an important exporter of textile products to the United States. The United States ships active ingredients for pharmaceuticals as well as the pharmaceuticals themselves, and Mexico ships pharmaceuticals.[12]

The trade results convincingly confirm the theoretical expectation. The most explosive growth in U.S.-Mexico trade in recent years has been intra-industry trade. Approximately 80 percent of Mexico's exports are now manufactured goods. Oil, which 15 years ago dominated Mexico's exports, constituted only 12 percent of the total in 1995. Mexico's reliance on the U.S. market has also grown as intra-industry trade thrived. In the early 1980s, the United States took 55 percent of Mexico's exports; in 1995, the proportion was 85 percent.

A related phenomenon is that the two-way trade is not only intra-industry, but also intra-firm and between parties related through strategic alliances. About 50 percent of Mexico's manufactured exports are of this nature, as are a comparable proportion of U.S. exports of manufactures to Mexico.[13] (The proportion of intra-firm trade between the United States and Canada is even higher.) Intra-firm trade stems mostly from U.S. investment in production in Mexico in the automobile, computer, pharmaceutical, and other industries. Foreign direct investment does not necessarily reduce U.S. exports, as critics of this investment assert, but frequently enhances it by permitting greater specialization. Canada is the country that receives both the greatest amount of U.S. FDI and the largest volume of U.S. exports. Mexico is among the leaders in U.S. FDI among the developing countries and by far the leading developing-country market for U.S. exports.

Trade in intermediate products.   Specialization and intra-industry and intra-firm trade across national boundaries has a number of consequences. One of the most important is that it encourages trade in intermediate as opposed to final products. An engine produced in Mexico and shipped to the United States for incorporation in a car assembled there (or vice versa with respect to where the engine is made and the car assembled) is trade in an intermediate product. So is trade in computer chips, as is much of the interchange in the products listed above that move in both directions. Shipping intermediate products—those that become inputs in the production of other goods and services—requires low barriers; otherwise the cost of shipping across national boundaries can become burdensome. Modern competitiveness depends heavily on the ability to produce anywhere for tapping the local market and specializing in a number of locations for incorporation of the output into more fully elaborated products elsewhere. This explains the support of U.S. business for NAFTA and for lowering trade barriers globally.

Mexico has the added advantage for the United States that it is close and transportation costs can be low. If just-in-time inventory practices are followed, Mexico and the Caribbean provide advantages over more distant locations, especially for bulky products. This practice of specialization, of producing parts of final products in a number of locations, is not just a U.S.-Mexican phenomenon. Japan invests heavily in this kind of production in East Asia and Western Europe increasingly in Eastern Europe. This practice can be bemoaned, but it is at the heart of what is referred to as globalization. It started before NAFTA and will continue on a worldwide basis with or without NAFTA. Multinational corporations have global activities—in marketing, in providing services, and in their production processes. Approve of it or not, that is the way it is. And there is no convincing evidence that this is adverse to U.S. or world welfare.

Mexico breaks down its merchandise import data into three categories—consumer goods, intermediate products, and capital equipment.[14] In 1995, a full 80 percent of these imports were intermediate products. Despite the decline in overall U.S. exports to Mexico in that disastrous year for the economy, Mexico's intermediate imports from the United States went up. The big drop was in consumer imports.

The maquiladora system.   The maquiladoras, the plants that have flourished on the Mexican side of the border for further elaborating U.S. inputs, are one example of this trade pattern. This program was initiated by the Mexican authorities in the late 1960s to provide employment for what was expected to be a flood of Mexican workers returning home after the United States terminated the *bracero* program (the agricultural guest worker program initiated during World War II) in 1964. The maquiladora initiative was based on two related considerations: the Mexican decision to permit imports of intermediate products in bond, that is, without payment of import duty, into the maquiladora plants; and the U.S. provision to levy its import duty on the returned product only on the value added outside the United States. Most of this Mexican value added is labor, which is obviously cheaper in Mexico, but also includes utility and related costs.

The maquiladoras are a system of coproduction, of producing the intermediate product in the United States and then completing the product in Mexico. The system flourished, especially in years of peso devaluation because this reduced the dollar cost of wages. By now, the roughly 2,500 maquiladora plants in existence employ upwards of 700,000 people. Imports by maquiladora plants in 1995 amounted to $26 billion and exports from them were $31 billion, or net exports of $5 billion.[15] The principal products imported by the United States from the maquiladora plants are motor vehicles and parts, television receivers, electric capacitors, apparel, electric motors and generators, and measuring and testing equipment.[16]

Based on U.S. import (as opposed to Mexican export) data, imports from all countries under harmonized tariff heading 9802.00.80, the principal classification under which maquiladora imports enter, were $58.7 billion in 1994, of which $22.9 billion were from Mexico. The U.S. content of imports under this tariff heading was 21.3 percent for all countries other than Mexico and 50 percent for imports from Mexico. In other words, Mexican maquiladoras used more than twice the U.S. components per dollar of U.S. imports than did comparable imports from other countries.[17] Many Mexicans criticize the maquiladora plants for precisely this reason—they use too few material Mexican inputs.

One earlier incentive under the maquiladora system, that the imports into the United States pay duty only on the foreign value added, will gradually cease to be an advantage for Mexican maquiladoras as all tariffs disappear under NAFTA. The maquiladoras in their original form will cease to have any reason for existence, but this does not mean that the plants will disappear. Mexico still provides advantages for coproduction for the U.S. market. Increasingly, this coproduction is taking place

away from the border. Indeed, in 1995, non-maquiladora merchandise exports increased more in percentage terms than did
those from the maquiladoras. Coproduction, greater specialization, is taking over most of the trade and not just the maquiladora trade set up specifically for that purpose.

Specialization: necessity and concern. What has been described in this section—the growth of specialization, of coproduction and trade in intermediate products—can be understood
in efficiency and competitive terms. At the same time, this phenomenon is at the heart of the uneasiness that surrounds NAFTA
on the part of labor unions and others concerned over the movement of production to Mexico to take advantage of less costly
labor. It is not enough to say that what is happening between the
United States and Mexico is happening elsewhere as well, because the Mexican experience is closer to home. It is evident,
however, that the kind of specialization that is occurring with
Mexico would continue even if NAFTA did not exist. In that
case, U.S. import duties on merchandise imported from Mexico
would not be zero, but would not be very much higher, in about
the 3 percent range on average. It is also not self-evident that
U.S. workers would benefit if U.S. producers and traders could
not re-import the elaborated products after shipping intermediate products to Mexico (and elsewhere). In this case, entire production operations might move offshore and U.S. workers
would not then produce even the 50 percent that they now do
under the maquiladora system.

   A lengthy survey article in the *Economist* in September 1996
deals with the worldwide concern about the effects of globalization. The opinion of the author of this article (Pam Woodall) is
that globalization and information technology are benefiting the
vast majority of humanity. The article points out that over the
past decade, trade has been growing twice as fast as output and
foreign investment three times as fast. A key sentence of the
review is the following: "The future prosperity of rich economies
will depend on their ability to innovate and on their capacity to
adjust to change."[18]

   The best way to deal with the undoubted concern that exists
about the direction that world production is taking is to continue
high job creation in the United States. This will not solve all
problems because the new jobs will not necessarily go to the
persons who are displaced by the changes in production that are
occurring. Yet, this shifting of production from location to

location, internally and abroad, will not be stopped by eliminating NAFTA. U.S. jobs will not be created on a net basis by burdening imports because this will prejudice other jobs—generally higher-skill and higher-paying jobs—by curtailing exports.

Some Sectoral Developments

The division of labor that is occurring between Mexico and the United States under NAFTA can be examined a bit more closely in the two sectors that were treated most problematically in the agreement. These are the automotive industry, the single most important sector in the two-way trade, and textiles and textile products. Each has restrictive rules of origin to protect producers in NAFTA. The rule in the automotive sector, omitting many of the complications, is that free trade requires North American value added of 62.5 percent for most vehicles; for textiles, the basic rule is referred to as yarn-forward, that is, an item must be made of yarn produced in the NAFTA countries to be eligible for regional preference.[19]

The automotive industry. The automotive industry is particularly sensitive to economic conditions, such as the level of real income, interest rates, and the availability of credit, and, in international trade, to shifts in exchange-rate relationships. It is not surprising, therefore, that there was a substantial contraction in domestic demand for automobiles and trucks in Mexico in 1995. The only reason the situation in the Mexican industry was not worse that year was the increase in exports to the United States: Mexico sold more automotive products to the United States in 1995 than it imported, the first time this had happened since 1989. Nonetheless, consistent with the position taken on bilateral trade balances generally—that they are an improper measure for judging the benefits of NAFTA—the change in a bilateral trade balance in a single sector in one or a few years is no way to measure the long-term consequences of the sectoral integration taking place.

Mexican production of cars and trucks for the domestic market dropped by 70 percent in 1995, some of which was offset by the 38 percent increase in exports, largely to the United States. Domestic demand recovered by about 50 percent in 1996 over the previous year, but during the first five months sales abroad represented 80 percent of vehicle production. Of the eight large companies that participate in the auto, light truck, and van market in Mexico, Chrysler was the most successful in expanding exports, most of which went to the United States.[20] Employment in the terminal and parts industries in Mexico fell in 1995 from 199,000 to 188,000, but then recovered to at least the earlier level by mid-1996.

According to the Bureau of Labor Statistics, employment in the U.S. vehicle and equipment industry in June 1966 was 965,000. This is actually an increase from the 821,000 reported at the end of 1993, that is, pre-NAFTA.[21] This has little to do with NAFTA. It has everything to do with the domestic economy and the increased competitiveness of the U.S. terminal and parts producers.

The U.S. Department of Commerce, whose main mission is to promote U.S. exports, approaches developments in automotive trade between the United States and Mexico from a mercantilistic perspective. The U.S. Congress specifically mandates that Commerce report this way based on how the automotive industry is faring under NAFTA. Thus, the emphasis in the Commerce report on the industry in 1995 was that while U.S. exports of motor vehicles to Mexico fell by 42 percent from the previous year, they were double the pre-NAFTA 1993 level.[22] The actual bilateral trade data reported for 1995 by Commerce were U.S. vehicle exports to Mexico, $394 million; parts exports, $6.7 billion; vehicle imports from Mexico, $7.8 billion; parts imports, $10.5 billion.

Consistent, however, with the argument throughout this study that import levels depend primarily on economic growth, U.S. auto sales to Mexico rose dramatically in 1996 as the Mexican economy recovered. Passenger vehicle exports during the first quarter of 1996 were 111 percent above those of the first quarter of 1995, and truck exports were 339 percent higher. The big three (General Motors, Ford, and Chrysler) shipped a record 26,553 vehicles to Mexico from U.S. and Canadian plants in the first five months of 1996, compared with 19,863 in the first five months of 1994 and only 10,574 in the same period of 1995.[23]

If the emphasis is placed not on the bilateral trade balance—because this will continue to change depending on the relative economic situations in the two countries—but instead on total automotive trade between the two countries, this was increasing before NAFTA and continued its rhythm of increase after NAFTA. Total two-way trade figures, combining vehicles and parts, were as follows in recent years: 1991, $13 billion; 1992, $16 billion; 1993, $18 billion; 1994, $23 billion; 1995, $25 billion.

U.S.-Canada automotive trade increased markedly after the 1965 auto pact between the two countries permitted more thorough integration of the industry. A similar integration, which started later, is in full swing between the United States and Mexico. It is now appropriate to talk of a North American auto market. The Department of Commerce in its first automotive report to the Congress made special note of the fact that, in 1995, U.S. companies used their Mexican production to supplement U.S. production of vehicles in high demand in the United States, especially sport utility vehicles.

Integration with Mexico is still not an overwhelming factor in the U.S. automotive industry. But it may well be one day, just as integration with Canada is today. Indeed, if the Mexican economy can manage to sustain GDP growth over an extended period, the Mexican connection could even surpass that with Canada, which has less than a third of Mexico's population. As the trade and production data show, U.S.-Mexican integration in this sector was occurring before NAFTA. It will take many more years before a meaningful assessment of NAFTA's contribution in this important industry can be made.

Textiles and products. The domestic social and political implications of changes in this industry are considerable because of its ubiquitous presence throughout the United States and the high level of employment it affords. Total U.S. employment in the mill sector in 1995 was 628,000 and in the apparel sector 856,000. This sensitivity is reflected in the restrictions that have long existed in trade in these sectors, epitomized by the Multifiber Arrangement (MFA), which is legally sanctioned in GATT, under which countries are permitted to impose quotas on imports by precise textile commodities. There was agreement in the Uruguay Round of GATT to phase out these quotas over 10 years, ending in 2005. This phasing out was end-loaded—delayed as long as possible—by the United States and other industrial countries. Many developing country exporters of textiles and products themselves impose quotas on their imports.

U.S. textile and apparel exports globally have increased consistently for at least the last 15 years. This is particularly true for textiles as opposed to apparel; textile exports in 1995 were $7.1 billion and apparel exports $6.5 billion. At the same time, the U.S. trade deficit with the world has been increasing. It was $38.1 billion in 1995, of which $34.9 billion was accounted for by apparel.

Mexico in 1995 took 13.5 percent of U.S. textile exports and 21.6 percent of U.S. apparel exports. In value terms, this amounted to $2.2 billion, of which $1.3 billion were apparel and $0.9 billion textiles. In value terms, this was 10 percent more than in 1994, which was 29 percent more than in 1993. Imports from Mexico, largely apparel, were $3 billion in 1995, an increase of 60 percent over 1994, which was 38 percent more than in 1993. Two-way trade, in other words, has been increasing; this ante-dates NAFTA, but there was a big leap in apparel imports from Mexico after NAFTA came into effect.

This requires some elaboration. Apparel imports from Mexico in 1995 amounted to 774.3 million square meter equivalents (SME). They rose further by 41 percent during the first quarter of 1996, making Mexico the number one source of imported apparel. Nearly 80 percent were what are called 807A imports, which means that because they are made from fabrics cut and formed in the United States, they get immediate duty-free treatment, rather than in 1998 when NAFTA's duty elimination on these products is fully phased in. They also enter the United States without quota restriction. Another 6 to 7 percent were 807 imports, that is, the fabric from which the apparel was made was formed in Mexico, although cut in the United States; these imports pay the duty on the value added in Mexico, and they are subject to quota only if the fabric was of non-NAFTA origin. The rule of origin was met by 94 percent of apparel imports from Mexico.[24] Maquiladora operations for the production of Mexican apparel have increased since the December 1994 devaluation because of the reduction in the dollar cost of peso-denominated wages.

U.S. imports of textiles and apparel from all sources grew by 6 percent in 1995, and apparel imports alone by 10 percent. The rise in apparel imports was from 8.4 billion SME in 1994 to 9.2 billion SME in 1995, and Mexico took a disproportionate share of this increase. The Mexican share rose further during the first quarter of 1996, apparently at the expense of other leading suppliers, such as the Caribbean Basin countries as a group and China and Hong Kong. The request for parity of treatment with Mexico that has been raised by the Caribbean Basin countries, which receive preferences in the U.S. market under the Caribbean Basin Initiative (CBI), is based primarily on competition for apparel exports to the U.S. market. The CBI countries have a system comparable to Mexico's "special treatment" (or 807A) known as "guaranteed access levels." Parity has not yet been achieved, but the issue remains very much alive.

Based on the data to date, there has been diversion in favor of Mexico to the detriment of other apparel suppliers exporting to the United States as a result of NAFTA preferences. This may be temporary, particularly as quotas under the MFA are eliminated and competition from low-cost producers elsewhere becomes more fierce.

NAFTA has been a force in determining textile trade. Mexico has benefited in terms of its increase in exports to the United States, but this has been based largely on fabric cut and formed in the United States. The rule of origin, coupled with the special regime for Mexican apparel, has been effective in raising the use of U.S. yarns, fabrics, and pre-cut and pre-formed products. If one looks only at what has been happening in trade between the United States and Mexico, it can be argued persuasively that NAFTA has been accomplishing its objective in this sector. Viewed more broadly from a world welfare viewpoint, the apparent diversion of trade away from other suppliers portrays a less benign picture. Much of what now exists may undergo considerable transformation, however, as the end of the MFA alters the system of quotas on which much world trade takes place in this sector.

The Downside of NAFTA

Two types of problems necessarily accompany free trade. The first has to do with the hardships created even as the agreement works as it should; the second, with what happens when special interests seek to prevent NAFTA from functioning as envisioned. Put another way, production shifts from one location to another or import increases that displace domestic products can lead to localized unemployment and wage contraction, and open markets often bring on efforts to restrict imports precisely to limit competition.

Localized Hardships

Although there is no evidence that significant U.S. job-creation has been prejudiced by NAFTA, job losses do occur in specific localities and industries as a result of import competition and shift of production to Mexico. Hardships of this type accompany all economic restructurings, as old industries recede and new ones take their places, or as technology makes old ways of producing obsolete. Most of these problems arise from shifts within the U.S. economy. New England went through a down period when textile mills moved to southern states. Computers largely replaced typewriters.

NAFTA is different from these internal changes because the production shifts and consequent increased imports come from foreign sources. Ross Perot and Pat Buchanan do not rail about Michigan losing auto jobs to Texas, which happened during downsizing at General Motors. Many California furniture makers moved production to the south in the United States, but this went unremarked—except for the workers and communities involved—whereas shifts to Mexico were featured prominently in the media. Jobs are lost when plants shut down or downsize whether this is due to imports or domestic considerations. Because of inherent xenophobia, however, much more attention is devoted to the growth of imports from, or the shift in production to, Mexico.

The perennial debate for dealing with the undoubted hardship created by changes related to foreign competition is whether to alleviate the hardship through import protection or by helping affected workers adjust to the new situation. Both solutions are used, neither very effectively. Import restrictions are costly and shift the burden to consumers or the taxpayers as a whole. Moreover, they rarely change the direction of change, as the United States learned in its costly protection against automobile imports from Japan. Protection that originally is touted to be temporary sometimes becomes quite durable, as has been the case for textiles and textile products. Adjustment assistance can also be costly, but, more to the point, it burdens the federal budget; it is much easier to shift the cost of import protection directly to the consumer. This is why so much attention is paid to the inefficient protectionist correctives against import competition. Beyond this, adjustment assistance does not always work; the timing is often bad or the people that most need it are in no position to take advantage of what is offered because of age or inability to move to another location.

There has been considerable reporting of the hardships brought on by NAFTA. One incident chosen more or less at random from the *Journal of Commerce* reported the closing by Pendleton Woolen Mills of two of its six U.S. apparel plants, one in Portland, Oregon, and the second in Council Bluffs, Iowa, with a reported combined loss of 163 jobs. The headline for the story read "Apparel workers stranded as plant moves to Mexico," and the subhead, "Employees at Pendleton Woolen Mills blame job losses on free-trade pacts such as the Nafta and GATT."[25] The story was datelined Portland and contained considerable human interest content about how the lives of relatively low-paid U.S. workers would be altered by the change. It is more difficult to write a human interest story about U.S. jobs that are created under freer trade because these benefits are more diffuse geographically and causally more indirect. Nor is there much interest in the U.S. media about the effects of these shifting patterns of production on the fate of workers in Mexico.

The hardship depicted in the story undoubtedly is real and is repeated almost daily as plants close in one place and move on to another. One can blame GATT or NAFTA, as such stories do; but the shifts in the textile industry long antedate NAFTA, and the history of the MFA in the GATT is one of slowing down the changes to the detriment of U.S. consumers and workers in poor nations. A point made earlier is worth repeating: Restricting imports for the benefit of a single sector is always a partial correction, the overall consequences of which are generally adverse and rarely captured by the media.

The problem needs no belaboring, but it is vexing because there is no simple or cost-free solution. Most economists favor adjustment assistance over import restrictions as the desired approach to dealing with the issue because the negative ripple effects can be contained. Because of budgetary implications, the political solution usually is to impose import restrictions because this permits shifting the immediate burden of adjustment to consumers and the ultimate burden to something more abstract, the economy as a whole. So we do much restricting and minimal adjustment assistance.

Import Restraints

The period since the end of World War II has been a golden era for the reduction of international trade barriers—or perhaps only silver, because many restrictions remain. One of the inevitable truths of this period of repeated negotiations in GATT to lower trade barriers is that as one restriction was removed, those affected by competition sought to replace it with another. The same barrier-removal/barrier-innovation combination is present in regional economic integration efforts. The entrepreneurial mind, abetted by trade lawyers, is highly adept at finding super-ficially plausible reasons for trade restrictions. One can always find a credible rationale for protectionism, but it is invariably par-tial. Unfair trade practices by others, low wages in exporting countries, buy national to create jobs at home, the need for time to adjust to foreign competition, satisfying some local constitu-ency—the list of excuses is endless.

NAFTA has not been exempt from this practice. The agree-ment is designed to remove most tariffs and other trade barriers over 10 years, 15 years for a few products, but there are many rearguard actions to override this central commitment. NAFTA, as meticulous analysts point out, is not fully a "free-trade" agreement, but the intent at the limit is free trade.

Because the effort to limit competition from foreigners is inevitable, agreements like NAFTA require mechanisms to settle disputes that erupt when restrictive action is threatened or taken. In many respects, the effectiveness of these agreements can be assessed by how expeditiously disputes are resolved. On the whole, the parties to NAFTA are living up to the commit-ments they made in the agreement. All three parties, however, stray from the straight and narrow from time to time. The dis-cussion will start with Mexico and then list restrictive U.S. actions.

Mexico. U.S. government documents cite the following re-strictive practices pursued by Mexico since NAFTA:[26]

- For products subject to technical regulations, Mexico has insisted on using national testing facilities that are still not adequate and has forced each importer to replicate test-ing even if another importer had arranged to test the same product. In March 1996, one problem was resolved by agreement for mutual acceptance of test data for new truck and automobile tires, but many other problems re-main. In the telecommunications field, for example, dead-lines were not met and standards were established in a general way, rather than in terms of network consistency.

- Mexico has established standards, including "emergency" phytosanitary standards, that impede the entry of U.S. grains, citrus, cherries, cling peaches, and Christmas trees.

- Although Mexico has committed itself to enforce a high level of protection for intellectual property, pirated versions of cassettes, compact disks, and videos with copy-righted material are readily available in Mexico.[27]

- Mexico has an extensive list of exclusions from the procurement permitted by Pemex and the Federal Electricity Commission (CFE), both government-owned entities whose procurement was to be significantly opened under the NAFTA agreement.

- Customs procedures are often changed with little advance notification.

More generically, procedural problems arise regularly. One frustration with respect to establishing standards is that regulations are promulgated with little opportunity for prior comment. In the case of textile products, regulations were written that required listing the country of origin for each component. The implementation of the regulation was delayed and then altered after exporters complained that this would impose a costly burden. The main complaint on the U.S. side is the lack of transparency and the main suggestion is that a more open process would reduce problems. Mexican authorities consult with the business community in Mexico, often competitors of the importers, but rarely with consumer groups. One of the most highly publicized cases dealt with small package delivery, which in effect kept United Parcel Service from using large trucks on Mexican highways to deliver many packages for later distribution in minivans for its courier service.[28]

Many of these issues are under regular consultation in various specialized committees established under NAFTA precisely to deal with such problems. In some cases, the Mexican restrictions appear to be designed to favor Mexican industries; this would seem to be the case for requiring each importer of the same product to retest. Large traders can get around this impediment by setting up their own trading companies in Mexico to be the importer of record, but this may not be feasible for small wholesalers and manufacturers. Other obstacles result from ultracaution, such as the requirement for a special certificate of origin to make sure that goods sold as "Made in the U.S.A." did not originate in China. This prevented many U.S. retailers from selling their full line of goods in Mexico.[29]

In the main, U.S. officials who deal daily with Mexican authorities believe that many problems arise from the inability to shed old habits. Until it began to open its economy in the

1980s, Mexico was noted for the lack of transparency in government actions. The import-substitution model under which Mexico functioned until about 10 years ago was designed to protect Mexican producers. Regulations were written based on this cozy government/private-sector relationship. Businesspersons and government officials were forced to consult with each other, but Mexican consumers were given short shrift. It is taking time for the old dogs to learn new tricks.

In one unfortunate respect, however, new protectionist tricks are being absorbed only too quickly. Before NAFTA, Mexico did not use antidumping (AD) and countervailing duty (CVD) measures to restrict imports. They really weren't necessary; Mexico had many other techniques for keeping out foreign goods, such as high tariffs and import licensing requirements.

Under NAFTA, each member country retains its own antidumping and countervailing duty laws and regulations. Mexico is now using these, especially AD actions. To qualify under chapter 19 of NAFTA, which establishes a panel system to appeal national AD and CVD actions, Mexico had to alter its legal procedures to make its decision-making in these areas open to outside scrutiny. As of mid-1996, four Mexican AD decisions against U.S. imports were under review under chapter 19 (cut-to-length steel, polystyrene glass, flat steel sheet, and steel tube).[30]

The United States is surely the world champion in the use of these so-called unfair trade practices (i.e., AD petitions against foreign dumping and CVD action against subsidized foreign exports). Mexico is still a novice, but learning.

United States. The literature on U.S. use of AD and CVD procedures is extensive and needs no repetition here.[31] As of mid-1996, four such appeals submitted by Mexico against the United States under chapter 19 were pending (ceramic kitchen appliances, cement, oil tubular products, and flowers; and one ruling in favor of Mexico had been completed, on leather).[32]

As an aside, one would expect that the logic of a free-trade area would be to treat product pricing matters between the member countries the same way they are treated within countries. Within the United States, predatory pricing is dealt with under business practice laws. Under NAFTA, it is not. A petitioner does not have to demonstrate predatory pricing to obtain a favorable AD decision and the imposition of a compensatory duty, but only that the product is sold in the United States at less than fair value. This is an abstruse term, one not easy to define, but one test is whether a product is being sold in the United States for less than at home, say, in Mexico. The shipment of a product from Ciudad Juárez just across the border to El Paso, Texas, is treated quite differently under the AD law from a shipment of the same product from San Antonio, Texas, to El Paso. Both the Mexicans and the Canadians, at different times, suggested that the handling of AD cases be made to conform with the way predatory pricing problems are handled within countries. The United States was unwilling to accept this, probably justifiably in the case of Mexico due to the primitive nature of its antimonopoly laws and regulations. Over time, however, the logic of a free-trade area—that pricing aspects be the same for internal and cross-border sales by any of the three NAFTA countries—may prevail.[33]

The highest-profile recent AD case in the United States was that brought by U.S. tomato growers against fresh tomato imports from Mexico. The case was significant because it involves considerable trade, about $450 million in 1995. One study of this case reached the following conclusion: ". . . none of the proposed measures [on restricting Mexican imports] actually addresses the fundamental question of how Florida growers can adapt to the evolving reality of globalization by increasing their competitiveness and/or diversifying."[34]

U.S. tomato growers had brought a second case, this one not under the AD provisions of U.S. law, claiming damage from imports and requesting temporary relief, which triggered an investigation under section 202 of the trade act of 1974. The U.S. International Trade Commission (ITC) concluded in August 1996 that fresh tomatoes (and bell peppers, which were part of the same investigation) ". . . are not being imported into the United States in such increased quantities as to be a substantial cause of serious injury, or the threat thereof, to the domestic industries producing articles like or directly competitive with the imported articles."[35]

The ITC had signaled this finding in a preliminary report a month earlier, in July, and this prompted an extraordinary and, to my knowledge, unprecedented, joint statement by U.S. Secretary of Commerce Mickey Kantor and U.S. Trade Representative Charlene Barshefsky that "we are very disappointed in today's decision."[36] The ITC was set up to gather evidence and hold hearings independently of political pressure from the administration. Failing this, there is no legitimate reason for the commission because, in that case, the president can make his own decisions with the advice of his political appointees and without the charade of the commission. The Kantor-Barshefsky statement makes clear how highly political the tomato case had become, particularly in Florida just before a presidential election.

The AD case was resolved without any final determination by either the U.S. Department of Commerce or the ITC. An agreement was reached under which Mexican growers consented to a floor price for tomato sales to the United States.[37] In reality, the Mexicans were bludgeoned into doing this. It was abundantly clear from the expression of disappointment of Commerce Secretary Kantor after the earlier ITC decision denying relief to the U.S. tomato growers that his department could hardly be judiciously neutral in this case.

Who is hurt by such action? The U.S. process for administrative fairness in dealing with such trade disputes is surely compromised. U.S. consumers will have to pay higher prices. Some of this windfall will go to the growers from each country, Mexico and the United States. It seems, especially in a political year, that the only U.S. constituency that must be forced to pay the piper is the consuming public.

Presidential politics seemed to dominate at least two other decisions. The first has to do with surface transportation. NAFTA specified that trucks from Mexico and the United States would be permitted to carry cargo to the contiguous states of the other country three years from the date of signature of the agreement. At the eleventh hour, on December 18, 1995, when the Interstate Commerce Commission was supposed to receive applications for trucks to haul cargo across the border, the United States announced unilaterally that it would delay this processing. The reason given was fear about the safety of Mexican trucks and insufficient training of Mexican drivers, even though there had been a number of years to deal with these concerns. It was evident to outside observers that the safety issues would not be resolved before the U.S. presidential election of November 5, 1996; and, of course, they weren't.[38]

The United States deliberately violated an agreement it had entered into, an egregious action for a country of laws. The United States would be furious, and with good reason, if Mexico had taken comparable action to unambiguously violate its legal obligation because it had to mollify a particular national interest, say, Mexican truck drivers.

The second action dominated by domestic politics was the failure, again at the eleventh hour, to lift the prohibition on avocado imports from Mexico. The ban on Mexican imports has been in existence for more than 80 years, based on sanitary considerations, namely, the fear of weevils, fruit flies, and other pests entering California from avocados imported from Mexico. Measures to eliminate the risk had been under discussion between experts from the two countries for a number of years, and the U.S. Department of Agriculture was satisfied and proposed to lift the ban, at the same time putting into effect a number of safeguards against infestation of the U.S. product. The delay in doing this was announced in August 1996, following highly publicized protests from the California Avocado Commission. The commission, which represents the growers, argued that the U.S. plan to open the market was based on flawed information. In practical terms, this meant that no Mexican avocados would be on grocery shelves in the United States for at least another year.[39] California was even more important in presidential electoral terms than Florida.

Assessing the Trade Evidence

By way of summary, a number of conclusions emerge from the evidence on how well NAFTA is functioning in its main purpose of stimulating U.S.-Mexico trade.

1. The most important and incontrovertible fact is that two-way trade has become quite substantial between Mexico and the United States. This is the main objective of NAFTA. When the Mexican economy grew in 1994, so did U.S. exports. When the Mexican economy faltered in 1995, so too did U.S. exports. This is precisely what one would expect. As the Mexican economy began to recover in 1996 from its economic catastrophe of the previous year, U.S. exports also resumed their growth.

2. Looking at the picture as it unfolded in Mexico, its export growth to the United States has been steady since NAFTA, as one would expect in years during which the United States did not have a recession. In 1995, the Mexican economic scene was disastrous enough, but it would have been much worse without the pickup in exports. This was the one bright development for Mexico that year. Mexico was out of reserves and portfolio

capital did not seek out Mexico. Under these circumstances, Mexico had no alternative but to reduce or eliminate its current account deficit; and it did so, thanks in
large part to its increased merchandise exports.

3. The breakdown of the composition of trade demonstrates that what the specialization theorists anticipated
would accompany economic integration did in fact
occur. This is a crucial aspect of competitiveness and
why countries seek to integrate with others. The contention that this specialization would lead to generalized
unemployment in the United States proved to be inaccu-
rate. There has been localized unemployment and dis-
placement, and assistance must be provided to alleviate
the hardship this causes.

4. There has been some fudging of the obligations of
NAFTA on the part of both Mexico and the United
States. It would have been surprising if there had not
been; an agreement of this type does not suspend the
instinct of self-protection and does not spell the end of
interest politics. On the whole, however, the two countries are meeting the commitments they entered into.

5. Perhaps the most important example of meeting its commitment was Mexico's handling of its balance-of-payments problem. Instead of following its earlier instinctive
practice of imposing across-the-board import restrictions, it instead used macroeconomic policy measures to
deal with its problems. The result was a severe depression, but Mexico's economy recovered more quickly than
it had after the 1982 crisis, and U.S. exports to Mexico
fared considerably better during this economic horror
than they had after the previous one.

4

Finance

The growth of trade between the United States and Mexico is substantial, steady, and almost taken for granted by now. Good, yes, but what else is new? The economic collapse in Mexico, which was an unexpected event, started with a well-publicized action, a devaluation of the peso in December 1994, which quickly mushroomed into a full-fledged liquidity crisis. This, in turn, led to the corrective policies that resulted in the drop of 6.9 percent in Mexico's GDP in 1995. And, in turn, this led to the drop in U.S. exports to Mexico and stimulated Mexican exports to the United States to compensate for the paucity of internal demand in Mexico.

The proximate trigger to the depression in Mexico in 1995 was the devaluation, but this was preceded by what we now know was misguided financial and monetary policy during the previous year. It is thus evident that financial issues cannot be separated from real ones, those related to the production and consumption of goods and services. But even this is too simple. The financial errors were compounded by some underlying developments, such as the low and declining rate of domestic savings that meant that Mexico had to rely excessively on foreign savings not only to finance its current-account deficit, but also to provide capital for domestic investment. One way to define a current-account deficit is that actual domestic savings are insufficient to finance a desired level of investment. There is no single and easily identified cause of the crisis, but rather an amalgam of many actions and shocks that all came together when (to use another metaphor) the cork was pulled on the exchange rate.

Any person even modestly sophisticated in international trade knows that an economic depression will dampen imports. In that case, there is not enough income to pull in extensive foreign goods and services, just as there is not enough income to sustain domestic demand. To simply point, therefore, to the shift in the bilateral trade balance to a Mexican surplus in 1995 without at the same time making clear that it arose from the economic situation in Mexico is misleading. Many opponents of NAFTA do precisely this.

The more relevant issue to examine is whether the economic collapse was brought on by NAFTA. A related issue is whether Mexico, after confronting its economic debacle, is on a path that can lead to sustained growth in the future. It is this, after all, that will largely determine the growth of trade that is the key objective of NAFTA.

Causes of the Mexican Economic Collapse

The devaluation that triggered the run on the peso came on December 20, 1994. In that year, Mexico's merchandise exports were close to $70 billion, about 18 percent of its GDP of $380 billion. In other words, domestic themes were the dominant ones in the health of the economy. NAFTA was important, but it could not by itself rectify domestic policy mismanagement. NAFTA could not be a panacea for all the woes of Mexico—nor can it be for the United States for that matter. The pre-NAFTA hype sometimes gave the opposite impression, but this does not alter the reality.

A Year of Shocks

Shocks, which by definition are unexpected, occurred with wicked regularity in Mexico during 1994. On day one of the year, there was an uprising in the State of Chiapas. The date was chosen precisely because the leaders of the Zapatista National Liberation Army (EZLN) knew that the eyes of the world would be on Mexico that day, the official beginning of NAFTA.[1] This is not the place to discuss the grievances of the indigenous population of that poor state, but there were many legitimate ones—all unrelated to NAFTA.[2] In the context of a financial discussion, the significance of the uprising was that it raised questions in the minds of investors about the political stability of Mexico.

Then, in March, Luis Donaldo Colosio, the presidential candidate of the PRI, was assassinated in Tijuana. Nothing of this nature affecting the almost certain next president had happened in Mexico since the late 1920s. Although the man who pulled the trigger was arrested, convicted, and jailed, the full story of the murder has yet to be determined. Theories abound: the drug traders did it, for reasons that have never been explicated; the dinosaurs of the PRI were responsible, for fear that Colosio would change the nature of presidential choice and the conduct of politics, as he had implied he would in a campaign speech; even Salinas was blamed, based on precisely the latter concern to preserve the PRI.

The financial implication of this event was substantial. Mexico's net foreign reserves had grown to about $29 billion by February 1994, due mainly to an inrush of capital based on high interest rates coupled with faith in Mexico's economic future. Much of this was portfolio capital—investment in Mexican stocks and bonds—which, by its nature, is volatile. Between mid-March, following Colosio's assassination, and mid-April, Mexico lost more than $10 billion of reserves.[3] The situation calmed down after that—for a while, until the next shock.

Can this be blamed on NAFTA? Perhaps the capital inflow can to the extent that the agreement, coupled with what was then thought to be correct macroeconomic policy, promised stability and growth, but surely the outflow had nothing to do with NAFTA. It would be an unacceptable stretch to blame the shock of an assassination on a free-trade agreement.

The Mexican authorities had some choices following the Colosio assassination and the capital outflow it prompted. They could have devalued the peso as a way of discouraging imports, especially of consumer goods, and promoting exports, but this had its own risk—that of prompting a further capital outflow, such as that which actually took place after the December devaluation. Monetary policy could have been tightened by raising interest rates sharply, but there was concern that this would weaken the already fragile commercial bank structure. In any event, the central bank concluded that the turmoil after the assassination was a one-time shock and that the situation would calm down on its own, which in fact it did.

The authorities chose another route that, at the end of the day, proved fatal. They stepped up the issuance of what are known as *tesobonos*, short-term peso debt with an exchange-rate guarantee. The increase in tesobono sales replaced the more traditional *cetes*, government debt without the dollar indexation. Instead of dealing with the exchange rate, investors in Mexican government debt were given an exchange-rate assurance. After the devaluation in December, what turned out to be critical was more the short-term nature of the tesobonos than the exchange-rate guarantee. But this gets ahead of the story.

Were these central bank and Treasury decisions related to NAFTA? The clear answer is no. There might have been some reaction outside the country that Mexico was stacking the deck in favor of its exports had it devalued the peso abruptly and excessively, but this was not a major consideration at a time when the complaint of informed observers was that the peso was becoming increasingly overvalued. During the years starting at the end of 1987, the peso was used as the anchor to hold down inflation. A devaluation would have spelled the end of this policy. One could argue that a devaluation of the peso would have been the right thing to do, but the timing right after a political murder was hardly propitious. One can second-guess the decision-making, but these fateful determinations were unrelated to NAFTA.

There was a further fall in reserves of close to $3 billion from mid-June to mid-July in the runup to national elections in August. The explanation given by the Bank of Mexico (Mexico's central bank) was that this had to do with the resignation, later reversed, of the Secretary of Gobernación (the appropriate U.S. term is Interior or Government) over what he saw as electoral shenanigans. The elections themselves could have been a disturbing event, but they went off smoothly: most observers, internal and external, stated that they were the cleanest elections in modern Mexican history (and perhaps the qualifying word "modern" is not needed). During this period, there were also some spectacular kidnappings, for which large ransoms were extracted.

None of these events was related to NAFTA. In any case, the reserves remained steady after the $3 billion fall in the June-July period. All indications were that the authorities had acted correctly in treating the Colosio assassination and some of the subsequent shocks as temporary events that should not trigger drastic macroeconomic policy changes.

Unfortunately, the shocks were not over. In September, José Francisco Ruiz Massieu, the general secretary of the PRI, was murdered in downtown Mexico City. His brother, Mario, who was the chief investigator in the case, resigned in November charging a cover-up by the government. Mario Ruiz Massieu was later charged with illicit enrichment and was detained by U.S. authorities in Newark for not declaring funds he had in his possession. The story gets complicated, but the details are not necessary for this discussion.[4] The plot involves millions of dollars in U.S. bank accounts of Mario Ruiz Massieu, unsuccessful Mexican efforts to extradite him, and the later arrest of Raúl Salinas, the brother of Carlos, for complicity in the murder and, subsequently, for illicit enrichment on a scale not dreamed of even by informed insiders.

Each of these developments—José Francisco Ruiz Massieu's murder and his brother's resignation and later flight to the United States—roiled the financial markets. (The charges against Raúl Salinas came later.) Reserves started to fall again in November and the Bank of Mexico attributed the loss of $3.7 billion to the denunciations of the government made by Mario Ruiz Massieu when he resigned his position that month. These details are provided here only to justify the statement that all were unrelated to NAFTA.

Even then the shocks were not over. There were reports in mid-December of renewed fighting in Chiapas and Zapatista takeovers of a number of government positions. The stories of Zapatista successes proved false, but they served to spook the financial markets before the truth was brought out. The Bank of Mexico attributed the loss of another $1.5 billion of reserves to this intensification of hostilities in Chiapas. On December 20, when Mexico devalued the peso, the Bank's reserves were down to $10 billion. Remember that they had reached a peak of more than $29 billion on February 15, 1994. None of the specific triggering events that led to the bleeding of Mexico's international reserves was related to NAFTA.

Even as Mexico had to confront this veritable plague of internal shocks during 1994, the U.S. Federal Reserve was raising interest rates repeatedly to prevent an increase in U.S. inflation. The latest of these came on November 15, when the Federal Reserve raised the federal funds rate by 75 basis points to its highest level since 1990. As U.S. interest rates increased, the United States became a more attractive country for placing money, thereby diminishing the lure of Mexico. The U.S. Fed must have been aware that its policy was complicating the Mexican financial situation, but it obviously was acting in what it thought was the best interest of the United States. The Mexican authorities undoubtedly would have wished NAFTA to have had more influence in U.S. monetary decision-making, but it did not.

The case that Mexico's financial and economic collapse was caused by NAFTA cannot be made by looking at the specific shocks, internal and external, and their consequences on

Mexican international reserves. One must look at the overall policies that were followed in order to substantiate this charge—if it
can be substantiated at all.

Essentials of Mexican Economic Policy

In 1987, well before NAFTA was even on the horizon and before
Salinas became president, the Mexican financial and monetary
authorities instituted a series of yearly agreements, or *pactos*,
designed to reduce inflation. Consumer prices had risen by 160
percent in 1987 (measured December over December), and the
pactos that began that year, and were renewed with modifications each year through 1994, were undertakings by the government, labor, and business to bring down consumer and
wholesale prices. The government committed itself to hold
down expenditures; labor to moderate wage demands; and business to limit price increases. The pactos were successful in their
primary goal; inflation in 1994 was 7.1 percent, the lowest level
in 22 years.

A key feature of the anti-inflation drive was to limit devaluations of the peso or, using the term of art for what was done, to
make the exchange rate the anchor of the anti-inflation program.
The peso was devalued sharply at the end of 1987 and then, over
the coming years, its value was depreciated slightly each day but
by less than the inflation. In essence, Mexico had a modified
fixed exchange rate that, later, was converted to a band within
which the peso was permitted to fluctuate. This is a relevant
point, as will be noted below. Even though the peso was under-
valued when the pactos started in 1987, most observers felt it
had become overvalued by perhaps 20 percent by mid-1994.
There had been voices within Mexico, plus economic opinion
from the outside, that Mexico should have acted earlier to lower
the value of the peso in relation to the dollar.

Critics sometimes refer to this handling of the exchange rate
as a feature of the "neoliberal" policies that Mexico pursued. By
neoliberal they mean a form of classical liberalism, namely, a
country open to imports and greater reliance on the market than
on detailed regulations or government ownership of businesses.
But using the exchange rate as the anchor against inflation is
hardly a tenet of classical liberals, who certainly would have preferred either a fixed rate under a gold standard or its equivalent,
or a floating peso. Classical liberals would never have endorsed

the incomes policy that Mexico used under the pactos to control the inflation; they would have preferred getting macroeconomic fundamentals right and then placing reliance on the market.

Whatever label one chooses to describe it, Mexico's exchange-rate policy was not an artifact of NAFTA. It was set in place well before NAFTA and was based on the conviction of Mexico's economic policy makers that controlling inflation was the country's number one objective. Mexico probably could not have devalued the peso by a significant amount in late 1993, when NAFTA was under debate in the U.S. Congress, but this was not really contemplated at that time.

The other great vulnerability of the Mexican program was the growing current account deficit, which in 1994 was almost $29 billion, or 7.7 percent of GDP. The deficit, measured as a proportion of GDP, was high although by no means unprecedented when compared with deficits of some of the Asian tigers over various periods of time.[5] The significance of this large deficit was that it made Mexico vulnerable to internal and external shocks that could disrupt the flow of volatile portfolio capital. And, as we have seen, Mexico had these shocks in spades in 1994. Whatever could go wrong, did go wrong.

Mexico's merchandise trade deficit, the major part of its current-account deficit, was $18 billion in 1994. Of this, only $3 billion was with the United States. The remaining $15 billion was divided fairly evenly between Western Europe and Asia. It is therefore inaccurate to blame NAFTA for the large trade deficit. NAFTA trade not only increased sharply in 1994, but the benefits were highly balanced in both directions.

Mexico felt forced to devalue the peso on December 20 because it was running out of reserves. Reserves had dropped from $12 billion on December 14 to the $10 billion on December 19, and there was no assurance they would not fall further. A meeting of the pacto members on December 19 ran into the early morning hours of December 20 and the devaluation was announced a few hours later. The form it took was a widening of the upper limit of the band by about 15 percent.

The devaluation was badly handled. It was an action taken in panic without all the accompanying measures that are typical of devaluations. These normally are borrowing foreign exchange to defend the new parity and enveloping the devaluation in a number of related budgetary and fiscal actions. For about half a day, the markets were calm, but then all hell broke loose. By the end of December 20, reserves had fallen to less than $6 billion. In the days and months ahead, the peso plummeted in value.

The other piece of the policy story that deserves mention is that starting after the Colosio assassination, tesobono sales sky-rocketed. When the devaluation occurred, the outstanding amount was about $30 billion, almost all short-term and all indexed to the dollar. If one measured Mexico's net reserves on the basis that the tesobonos were short-term dollar obligations, which in fact they were, Mexico had negative reserves of $25 billion when the devaluation occurred. The facts about outstanding tesobonos could have been known to the market, but the evidence is that little attention was being paid. The facts about the precise decline in reserves were not known because the Bank of Mexico divulged these figures only quarterly.

Governments generally meet maturing obligations by refinancing. The sequence of events leading to the Mexican devaluation was such that holders of tesobonos were unwilling to provide the funds for refinancing. Instead, they wanted to cash these in. It was this that converted a devaluation crisis into a debt crisis. Mexico could not meet its short-term obligations. It was also nearly impossible to negotiate a debt rescheduling because, unlike the situation in 1982 when banks held most of Mexico's dollar debt, there were thousands of tesobono holders whose pension funds were invested in these instruments.

The foregoing details, while they could be extended, provide an ample picture of how Mexico got into the financial crisis and permit a judgment on the role of NAFTA in this process. The *only* argument one can make for any connection with NAFTA is to say that the capital that flowed into Mexico would not have done so without the agreement. This is tantamount to saying that the United States and Mexico made a mistake by helping to build market confidence in Mexico. The market was also sending funds into other emerging markets where there was no NAFTA.

The ineluctable conclusion must be that NAFTA played no role in the specific shocks that plagued Mexico in 1994 or in the financial debacle that struck the country at the end of the year. What turned out to be faulty financial measures is what did Mexico in, but NAFTA articles deliberately exclude coordination of national macroeconomic policy. NAFTA is a free-trade area, not an economic-monetary union of the type now contemplated by the European Union under the Maastricht Treaty.

Handling the Crisis

What began as a financial debacle soon became an economic crisis as well. There was nothing in the NAFTA agreement that specified how twin problems of this magnitude should be handled, but there was in fact cooperation on this score between Mexico and the United States. The U.S. contribution was a $20 billion credit, with the imposition of accompanying conditions on macroeconomic measures that Mexico had to take. These conditions conformed to what the Mexican authorities themselves thought were necessary. What follows deals with this and related credits, especially that from the International Monetary Fund (IMF), and how Mexico has fared over the two years since. The credit was immediately labeled the "Mexico bailout," but the rescue affected much more than Mexico. Its motive was also to avoid a crisis in the international monetary structure, one that would surely have adversely affected the United States as well if it had been allowed to run its destructive course without outside assistance.

The $20 Billion U.S. Credit

The United States was slow to react to the Mexican crisis, in part because it was not evident at first how negative the market reaction would be to the combination of devaluation and illiquidity. A case can be made that the fallout would have been far less had the United States and the international community reacted more quickly and thereby given a signal of support to the market. However valid that contention might be, that is not what happened. There was also a problem that the U.S. Treasury Department was without leadership at that moment; Lloyd Bentsen had resigned and Robert Rubin was not yet confirmed.

The support package that came early in 1995 consisted, in principle, of more than $50 billion, made up of $20 billion from the United States, $17.8 billion from the IMF, $10 billion in short-term swap facilities from a number of central banks channeled through the Bank for International Settlements (BIS) in Basle, Switzerland, up to $1 billion from Canada, and smaller sums from other countries in Latin America. The words "in principle" were used because not all these funds were drawn down. They were the insurance policy. The most important of these facilities were the support from the United States and the IMF. In each case, they were the largest support loans of this type ever provided from either the U.S. Treasury or the IMF.

The Clinton administration first sought legislation from the Congress to provide up to $40 billion in loan support. This was endorsed by the Republican leaders of the House and Senate, Representative Newt Gingrich and Senator Bob Dole. The proposal nevertheless ran into trouble, and when it became clear that it would not be approved, the legislative package was withdrawn and $20 billion was provided through the Exchange Stabilization Fund (ESF). The ESF, set up in the 1930s, was designed to do what its name implies, to support the dollar in international exchanges. Its facilities were normally of a short-term nature, like currency swaps that are intended to be reversed fairly quickly. The ESF never had been used for support as large as that provided to Mexico.

There was considerable criticism within the United States of the loan and the way it was handled. There was also some criticism from Mexican sources, but more on that later. The term "bailout," intended by the loan's critics to be pejorative, in the end seemed to be taken as merely descriptive. The main charge was that the credit was equivalent to pouring money down a rathole. Looking back, the more important issue is whether it worked. The answer is an almost unequivocal "yes."[6]

The total amount disbursed to Mexico under the U.S. $20 billion loan facility was $13.5 billion, of which no more than $12.5 billion was outstanding at any one time. In August 1996, Mexico prepaid $7 billion, leaving the amount then outstanding at $3.5 billion; and this was liquidated in January 1997. The prepayments were made possible by Mexico's borrowing longer-term money in international markets, a normal technique for loan repayments. The United States received about $500 million more in interest from Mexico than it would have under going interest rates on domestic paper of these maturities.

What options did Mexico and the United States have at the time the loan was made? Mexico had almost completely run out of reserves and had almost $30 billion in short-term tesobonos that had to be repaid and could not be refinanced. Mexico actually tried on several occasions after the devaluation to float new tesobonos to retire the expiring ones, but there was little interest from buyers at the auctions except at exorbitant interest rates. Mexico thus had two options: find funds wherever it could for an orderly payment of the expiring tesobonos, or default. The long-term price of reneging on government obligations would have been profound. This could have locked Mexico out of world money markets for years, and the cost in protracted depression in Mexico would have been immense.

There was criticism in Mexico of the loan. One complaint was more nationalistic than substantive, namely, that oil-export proceeds were used as collateral for the outstanding amounts and, according to the critics, this meant that Mexico had lost control of its oil revenues. It is not clear whether these critics believed that a $20 billion credit should have had no collateral. The proceeds from oil sales were passed through an escrow account in the Federal Reserve Bank of New York for payment to the U.S. Treasury in the event Mexico missed a loan repayment. As of the end of September 1996, $13.5 billion had passed through this escrow account and there were no set-offs against these.

The second criticism had more substance. This was that the loan was used to repay the holders of tesobonos, both Mexican and foreign, with the full foreign-exchange guarantee. This objection was raised in the United States as well. After all, investors had put their money in tesobonos because the return was higher than they could get at home. The rules of the market should have been that the players take their losses with their gains. They did not, and this raised what is known as moral hazard, namely, whether governments should make investors and speculators whole. This is a valid argument, but it was not easy to find a way of helping Mexico without raising the moral hazard issue. Many Mexicans believe that the $20 billion loan was approved *only* to pay off the investors. This comment lacks grace. This contention omits what the cost for Mexico would have been had there been no loan.

The United States, like Mexico, also had two options: to let nature—in this case, the market—take its course, or to intervene with the rescue package. Apart from the hardships it would have inflicted on Mexicans, the danger of the first option was that it would roil the entire monetary system and pose a greater danger than making the loan. Alan Greenspan, the chairman of the Federal Reserve Board, supported the loan on this basis, as did the Robert Rubin, the secretary of the Treasury. In its way, so did the international financial community, as evidenced by the IMF and BIS credits.

Both the IMF and Treasury loans imposed conditions on Mexico's fiscal and monetary policies, and these led to a harsh adjustment program, as discussed in the next section. The adjustment was sharp and this brought out the classic argument of gradualism versus shock treatment. The choice was in favor of rapid and not gradual adjustment.

The loan, to repeat, was not required by NAFTA. Was it influenced by the existence of the agreement? I suspect that it was. The United States had provided short-term funds to Mexico during previous crises, in 1976 and again in 1982. Indeed, the swap network among the central bankers of the industrial countries is a form of short-term rescues during particularly difficult moments, and these have become fairly routine. But never before was there a rescue as large as that for Mexico this time. Had Mexico been allowed to default, this could well have ended NAFTA.

While I suspect that the existence of NAFTA had something to do with the size of the credit, it is only fair to add that the magnitude and suddenness of the crisis also dictated that the amount had to be large to convince markets that Mexico could meet its expiring obligations. The concern over the impact of the financial crisis on the international monetary system was at least as great as concern over NAFTA's future. Neither the IMF nor the BIS took NAFTA into consideration in their credit lines.

Should the credit, even if it was successful in achieving its purpose, be chalked up as a plus for NAFTA or as a negative? Supporters of the agreement will take one side, opponents the other, that the credit should never have been granted. Does this matter any more? Probably not for the Mexican case, but it does have relevance for other cases in the future. The credit accomplished its purpose and the NAFTA connection, if any, is now the stuff of debating games and not practical policy.

The underlying reality of Mexico's tribulation is that it was caused by massive movements of capital into Mexico and then, at a moment of instability, out of Mexico—and the possibilities for this to recur elsewhere are only growing greater. The more germane policy issue has to do with the precautions taken by the international community to reduce the danger of similar financial crashes in individual countries and to be in a position to respond in a coordinated way much more quickly than was done in the Mexican case.

The Mexican Stabilization Program

The technical details of Mexico's stabilization program had to do with limiting public-sector spending and curtailing growth in

the net domestic assets of the Bank of Mexico. It was an ortho-
dox program of retrenchment to deal with rising inflation and
eliminate the deficit in the current account of the balance of
payments. Looking back more than a year later, the program
worked, but the price was exceedingly high.

The year 1995 was a horror for Mexico. GDP fell by 6.9 percent. Unemployment and underemployment data in Mexico are
not fully reliable, but there is no doubt that both rose substan-
tially. Open unemployment in urban areas rose from about 4 percent at the end of 1994 to more than 7 percent at the end of 1995.
Across the economy as a whole, unemployment rose by about
one million people in an economically active population of about
38 million. By one measure, underemployment increased by
about four percentage points during the year to about 18 percent.
Real wages in manufacturing and in wholesale and retail activities in major metropolitan areas fell by close to 20 percent.[7]

Bankruptcies soared as sales plummeted. Investment fell by
more than 30 percent during the year. All sectors felt the effects
of the depression, construction perhaps above all others, with a
fall of more than 20 percent. Retail sales declined by some 15
percent. Most home mortgage interest rates are tied to inflation,
and these soared. Consumer credit, particularly for automobiles, is similarly indexed. Consumer prices during 1995 rose by
52 percent. The government stepped in to alleviate some of the
hardships inflicted by these soaring interest costs, but there were
insufficient resources to resolve all problems.

Bank credit more or less ceased as nominal interest rates
went through the ceiling, exceeding 100 percent for some types
of consumer loans. Some 30 percent of outstanding loans (or
more, depending on how this is calculated) were delinquent.
The government also had to intercede to rescue banks, which
were in weak condition even before the catastrophe hit. The
restructuring of Mexico's banks is continuing and the final cost
will exceed 10 percent of GDP.

The figures can be mind-numbing, but there are human
interest stories behind them. Hardships during such a drastic
stabilization are never equally shared. Wealthier families have
greater ability, and more resources, to cope. Most middle-class
incomes plummeted in real terms, and it became routine for people to hold two or more jobs and for women to go or return to
work to augment family incomes. The informal economy grew,
much of it hawking items on the streets. Crime rates, especially

mugging, soared. It became routine for Mexicans to avoid hailing roving taxicabs because passengers were often taken to locations where confederates were waiting to seize their cash and force withdrawals from ATMs—or worse, in terms of physical beatings.

Yet the stabilization medicine accomplished its purpose. By mid-1996, it was clear that the economy was in recovery. Industrial production picked up, unemployment went down, and the overall growth rate for 1996 was 4.5 percent. The peso remained steady for much of 1996, even with little direct intervention by the central bank to accomplish this. The stock market recovered to its highest levels ever measured in peso terms. By mid-1995, Mexico was able to borrow money in international money markets, whereas after the 1982 collapse this was not possible for many years. Interest payments on borrowings were high, some 400 basis points above comparable rates for borrowings by industrial countries at first, but this is what one would expect when risk is perceived to be high.

Could the policymakers have accomplished a similar recovery with less hardship? This is the shock treatment versus gradualism argument. Politicians in Mexico, including (or perhaps especially) those from the PRI, would have preferred a more gradual process. Economists argue that the hardships of gradualism are even more severe, because they endure longer, and that in the end some shock therapy will be required in any event. There was criticism of the IMF and Treasury conditions for insisting on shock treatment, but the reality is that this was the approach also favored by the key Mexican policymakers.

The PRI, at its national assembly in September 1996, put in place requirements that its presidential and gubernatorial candidates had to have been party members for at least 10 years and to have held prior elective office. This was an expression of dissatisfaction with the performance of the technocrats.

This detail has been provided not because anything that was done to stabilize the economy was called for under NAFTA, but because the stabilization program took place in the second and third years of NAFTA operations. NAFTA did not cause the collapse and did not dictate the remedy, but this does not prevent critics of the agreement from blaming it.

Looking Ahead

The debt (tesobono) crisis that proved so devastating in the end was anticipated by no one, at least no one on record in print. The severity of the fallout was equally unexpected. For these two reasons—the speed with which the financial crisis turned into a debt crisis and then an economic debacle, and the anguish that the correction caused—some observers call what happened the first financial crisis of the twenty-first century. By this, they have in mind the fluidity of capital in today's world. Future crises are unlikely to follow the identical pattern, but the generic problems caused by the mobility of immense amounts of capital are now with us.

The Mexican experience thus leads to two kinds of questions. The first, and most relevant for the discussion in this volume, is what will happen to the Mexican economy in the years ahead. The second and more systemic question is how the international community as a whole will deal with future crises.

On the second point, funds available to the IMF to meet such crises have been increased. Publication of timely economic and financial information by member countries of the IMF has been generalized. Individual countries are now keenly aware of the price of misplaced macroeconomic policy and, for a while at least, one can expect greater caution. It is clear that the international capital markets are relentless and the consequences of errors are magnified.

The Mexican economy has had its workout, and a harsh one indeed. In addition to the stabilization program, legislation now has been enacted to alter the pension system to permit individuals to make their own investment decisions, and this should help increase national savings once the new system is in place. Mexico will surely be leery in the future about allowing its current account deficit to get too large or permitting the bunching of maturities of its public debt.

Barring political instability, there is no reason why Mexico cannot achieve steady growth in the future in the neighborhood of 4 to 5 percent a year. The structure for this growth is in place in its trade arrangements and production relationships. If national savings do increase, as the authorities hope will happen from the altered pension system, this will reduce the need to rely on volatile foreign capital to fill the investment void. The next few years should be reasonably favorable for Mexico. And, if so, U.S. exports there will grow as well.

The next danger point most likely will be at the end of the Zedillo administration in 2000. The financial crises of recent decades have come in six-year increments. If foreign investors think this will happen again, they will remove funds in advance for prudential reasons. Mexico, therefore, has about three years to convince the money managers that the next time will be different. This may be the major task as one looks ahead. The existence of NAFTA and the booming trade this has generated will not by itself change investor expectations, but it should help.

5

Institutions and Interactions

The smooth functioning of an agreement like NAFTA requires an institutional structure. NAFTA has provisions dealing with trade in goods and services, government procurement, investment, finance, intellectual property, telecommunications, and dispute resolution. There are two parallel agreements on environmental and labor cooperation. Circumstances change in all these fields, new situations must be addressed, and conflicts flare up. If NAFTA were unable to deal with this dynamism, the agreement would become redundant. Above all, the players from the private and public sectors of the three countries must develop familiarity with one another and with the idiosyncrasies of doing business in each other's environment.

As regional trade organizations go, the institutional structure of NAFTA is quite primitive. There is no monster bureaucracy, such as the Commission of the European Union (EU). There is a free-trade commission with headquarters in Mexico City, but it meets irregularly, as often as not to prevent disagreements from becoming major conflicts. This commission has no independent authority to make proposals, as does the EU commission, but instead is completely a creature of the three trade ministries. The choice of a minimal bureaucratic structure was deliberate to avoid even a minor intimation of supranationality.

There are, however, committees, working groups, and commissions—the distinctions among them are not always sharp—that meet regularly in their specific fields. There are also auxiliary bodies to deal with environmental and infrastructure financing. These groups work with little fanfare and are largely unknown, except to those who have an interest in the particular work being done.

A binational commission made up of cabinet officers from the United States and Mexico meets annually. The participation has increased during the past few years after NAFTA came into existence. Parliamentarians from the two countries have been meeting each year for many years, although, unlike the meetings of cabinet officers, this has become quite moribund.

On a broader scale, the NAFTA negotiations and operations spawned fundamental changes in the way the three nations do business with one another. For Canada, joining with Mexico in NAFTA began a process of discovery of a country about which Canadians were largely ignorant. This discovery is leading to increased trade and much new Canadian investment in Mexico. For example, Canadian banks have become players in the Mexican economy.[1] Even if its critics were to force the United States to terminate NAFTA, the Canadians would continue their free-trade relationship with Mexico because the private sector sees this as beneficial;[2] and this combination of withdrawal (by the United States) and continuation (by Canada) would result in discrimination against the United States in Canada-Mexico trade.

The focus here is on U.S.-Mexico relations. Mexico dramatically altered the way it operated in the United States when the NAFTA negotiations got under way. Before that, Mexico's External Relations Secretariat (SRE) was almost the only government agency operating in the United States. The Mexican embassy in Washington operated almost exclusively through the State Department. Embassy officials rarely saw members of the U.S. Congress, or even substantive officials in other U.S. executive agencies. This was an outgrowth of the traditional Mexican attitude of noninterference in the internal affairs of other countries. The reasoning was that if Mexico behaved in this discreet way in Washington, so too would the United States in Mexico City. The thinking was naive. The U.S. embassy has long had more people from other agencies than from the State Department, and they fanned out all over the Mexican governmental structure.

Mexico, before NAFTA, did little lobbying in Washington. Lawyers were hired when necessary to deal with trade cases before the courts and administrative agencies, such as the International Trade Commission, but Mexico did not use public relations firms. Attacks on Mexico thus went largely unanswered except for embassy and SRE press releases that hardly anybody read. The Mexican government does lobby today, mostly using embassy personnel, but also using U.S. professionals. This was abundantly evident when the U.S. debate on NAFTA's approval turned ugly in 1993. Mexico now sends blockbuster cultural exhibits to the United States—such as "Mexico: Splendors of 30 Centuries," during 1990 and 1991, and the exhibit of Olmec art of ancient Mexico at the National Gallery of Art in Washington in

1996—as a way of proudly demonstrating the nation's long, rich, and diverse history. Mexico, in other words, has adopted practices in the United States long used by other countries.

The NAFTA negotiations led to other institutional changes. The Mexican ministry dealing with trade, the Secretariat for Trade and Industrial Development (SECOFI), set up its own shop to direct the negotiations in Washington. The embassy in Washington now has experts from the responsible ministries to deal directly with U.S. counterparts on such sensitive issues as narcotics and migration. The Mexican government, in other words, operates in the United States much as the United States operates in Mexico, even if on a lesser scale.

Institutional Development

The following sections provide information on the institutions that exist to facilitate the implementation of NAFTA. The significant consideration is that they provide a mechanism for keeping up with the dynamism that exists in the commercial and financial interchange between the two countries. They also provide points of contact in each government for private actors who need information and assistance in the conduct of their activities.

Committees and Working Groups

There are now 24 committees and working groups under NAFTA and in each case their duties correspond to a particular clause of the agreement. The committees, and their subcommittees, deal with trade in goods and agricultural products; used clothing; sanitary and phytosanitary measures and the use of pesticides in agriculture; and standards for industrial products, land transportation, automotive products, and telecommunications. There are separate committees on financial services and to advise on handling private commercial disputes.

The working groups deal with rules of origin; customs problems; agricultural subsidies and marketing standards; competition matters; temporary entry of technical and managerial personnel under the agreement; emergency actions; government procurement; and services and investment.

The committees and working groups are staffed in all three countries by officials from the responsible agencies—in the United States these are USTR, Commerce, Agriculture, EPA,

Transportation, Justice, Treasury, and State. The three governments would interact with each other even without these committees and working groups, but the contacts would be more
sporadic and the get-togethers almost exclusively to deal with
problems.

The more organized arrangement encourages efforts to
avoid problems. This does not mean they always succeed.
Despite the Land Transportation Standards Subcommittee, the
United States, at the last moment, aborted the commitment it
made in NAFTA to permit trucks coming from Mexico to circu-
late freely in the four U.S. border states. The reason given was
concern over the safety standards of Mexican trucks.

Relations between U.S. officials and their counterparts in
most industrial countries, including Canada, have long been
quite fraternal. It was routine for them to speak with each other
by long-distance telephone on upcoming issues or problems.
This flexibility did not exist between U.S. and Mexican officials
before the NAFTA negotiations. It does now and telephone discussions and e-mail messages between Mexicans and Americans
are now common.

Dispute Settlement

NAFTA has a number of provisions for resolving disputes, and
they require institutionalization if they are to be effective.[3] The
most highly publicized is that of chapter 19 of the agreement,
which permits review of national antidumping and countervailing duty decisions. This provision required setting up a roster of
panelists who could serve when any country wished to lodge a
complaint against AD and CVD decisions of any of the others.
The mechanism is to establish five-person bilateral panels whose
decisions are final, subject only to an extraordinary challenge to
be heard before a panel of three sitting or retired judges from the
countries involved in the dispute. Chapter 19 has been invoked
often, as discussed in chapter 3. The mechanism is not without
its critics, particularly because it substitutes a panel system for
the normal judicial appeals process. Its relevance in this discussion is that it has institutionalized a process to resolve disputes
more quickly.

Chapter 20 of NAFTA also instituted a panel process for
dealing with disputes relating to charges that treatment by one
of the parties violates a provision of the agreement, or could violate it by a proposed law or regulation, or adopts policies that

nullify expected benefits. Once again, an institutional framework is established for dealing expeditiously with these complaints.

NAFTA has separate provisions for dealing with disputes relating to financial services, investment, the environment, and setting of standards, and the agreement also encourages the use of arbitration to settle private commercial disputes.

Environment and Labor

The United States insisted on supplemental agreements to NAFTA, the North American Agreement on Environmental Cooperation (NAAEC) and the North American Agreement on Labor Cooperation (NAALC). Two separate commissions were established, the Commission for Environmental Cooperation (CEC), with headquarters in Montreal, and the Commission for Labor Cooperation (CLC), located in Dallas. Each is an innovation in trade agreements, and each has spawned consideration of these issues in other trade agreements, such as the World Trade Organization.

The proponents of inclusion of these supplemental agreements argued they would force attention on these issues in the conduct of trade and investment in North America. The opponents argue that although international consideration of environmental issues and protection of worker rights are legitimate issues, their connection with NAFTA could lead to additional trade restrictions. This disagreement is quite intense and apparently held up approval of fast-track legislation to permit the United States to negotiate effectively for free trade in the Western Hemisphere.

The purpose here is not to enter into a detailed discussion of the validity of these two agreements in the NAFTA context, or even of the effectiveness thus far of the two commissions. Rather, the intent is to note the further institutionalization that is taking place in North American economic interactions as a consequence of NAFTA.

There has been both praise and criticism of the operations of the two commissions. The argument was made at the outset of this publication that the time elapsed since NAFTA has been in effect is much too short to reach definitive conclusions. A djust-ment of economies to new trading parameters takes mor three years. The case is even stronger that there has no enough time to assess the effects of the two new commi they were started later, and they are new and contentious ventures in international cooperation dealing with international trade and production.

It is thus not surprising that the early evaluations tend to be one-sided. The Public Citizen assessment, perhaps the most negative in the environmental field, makes the case that previous trends of environmental damage at the border were not arrested after NAFTA and the CEC came into existence.[4] Another publication states that the major criticism of the CEC comes from those U.S. and Canadian environmentalists who had a vision of a supranational body forcing governments into adopting new standards.[5] The premise of the CEC is that each country will enforce its own laws and regulations. The CEC argues that the environmental supplemental agreement offers the scope to argue competing trade and environmental values before dispute-settlement panels.[6]

The first national project selected for examination by the CEC concerned the damage that would result from a pier for cruise ships on the Mexican resort island of Cozumel. The Mexicans accepted the examination, but with some annoyance on the grounds that the project started before NAFTA came into existence. The CEC has an ongoing study to monitor the actual effects of increased trade and production on the environment, rather than to base all contentions on isolated anecdotes that are then extrapolated into alleged data.

The CLC was even slower than the CEC in getting organized. Its premise is that putting a spotlight on adverse labor practices will help improve the situation. Perhaps. The CLC has examined a number of cases, one on the Sony company's roadblocks to unionization of an electronics plant at the border, and another about the July 1994 closing by Sprint of a facility in California on the eve of a union representation election. Neither case has led to any penalty action by the CLC.

Border Environmental Bodies

Two other institutions merit mention, the Border Environment Cooperation Commission (BECC), headquartered in Ciudad Juárez, Mexico, and the North American Development Bank (NADBank), with headquarters in San Antonio. The BECC is intended to promote environmental cooperation at the U.S.-Mexican border and to certify projects for environmental improvement to make them eligible for financial assistance from the NADBank. The border in these agreements comprises 3,300 kilometers from the Gulf of Mexico to the Pacific Ocean, running 100 kilometers north and south of the frontier. The NADBank gets its funding from modest paid-in capital by the two governments and callable capital that serves as an ultimate commitment, if needed, when the Bank goes to the market to borrow funds.[7]

The two institutions were slow to get started. The NADBank also faces the major impediment that the border communities that most need infrastructure lack the financial autonomy and wherewithal to finance their part of projects or to repay loans. In essence, therefore, these communities must rely heavily on federal and state governments for financing at a time of restricted budgets. The major conclusion of a U.S. General Accounting Office study on this issue is that the infrastructure needs of the border continue to be unmet.[8]

The BECC and the NADBank are noteworthy for the same reason as the other institutions mentioned here. They, like the others, are in their infancy. They can be criticized for what thus far are modest accomplishments, but their very existence is the result of NAFTA and, in their case, recognition of an unmet environmental infrastructure need at the U.S.-Mexican border. Officials in Washington, D.C. and Mexico City paid little attention to border needs before NAFTA. This has now changed, although whether enough is hard to say. Be that as it may, attention and cooperation are the necessary first steps to environmental and infrastructure accomplishment in this most delicate region where the two countries come together.

NAFTA and Democracy

There is a correlation between market economics and democracy, but it is by no means perfect. Although all democracies are market economies, not all market economies are democracies. NAFTA, in its essentials, is undeniably a market-based agreement. One question that arose at the time of the ratification debate in the United States was whether the agreement would stimulate democratic development in Mexico.

Elections

The answer is not wholly clear. Mexico has made considerable advances in democratic norms, especially in electoral matters, during the three years that NAFTA has been in force. But, then, progress in this direction was being made before NAFTA. During 1996, electoral reforms deepened, but the causation probably came mainly from the economic and social debacle of 1995, which stimulated a national yearning for greater choice.

The EU has a condition that a country must be democratic before it can become a member. The entries of Spain and Portugal were delayed on this score. In MERCOSUR, the customs union among Argentina, Brazil, Paraguay, and Uruguay, the unmistakable message to Paraguay during 1996 was that if a budding military coup took place, the trade benefits it received from the agreement would be suspended. The issue in Mexico has not been retrogression in democratic practices, but the speed of political opening; but retrogression, if it did occur, undoubtedly would put the economic relationship with the United States in jeopardy.

There were modifications in democratic procedures during the six-year term of Carlos Salinas, from 1988 through 1994. The first governorship that the PRI conceded to the opposition after it came to power in 1929 was to the National Action Party (PAN) in 1989. By 1996, the PAN held four governorships. The PRI lost no federal senatorial contests until the Salinas years. The electoral laws were changed to give the opposition more seats in the federal Chamber of Deputies than it held earlier. With rare exceptions, the mayors of cities were *priistas* (supporters of the PRI) before Salinas and during his administration, but more opposition mayors were accepted during his *sexenio* (six-year term). Despite these modest democratic advances, it was explicit policy under Salinas to open the economy first, then (slowly) to turn to political opening. *Perestroika sí, glasnost no!*

By contrast, the political changes under President Ernesto Zedillo, who took office on December 1, 1994, have been extensive. The electoral law and procedures were worked out among the three major parties. Honest elections, of course, can be frustrated, but the mechanisms for assuring fairness exist. In elections in the state of Guerrero in early October 1996, the PRI won 54 of 76 municipalities but lost 12 mayorships it had held previously. The Guerrero contest was watched closely because the state has a history of violence, some occuring not long before the elections.

It is now considered conceivable that the PRI will lose its majority in the Chamber of Deputies in the 1997 legislative elections. It is no longer unthinkable that a non-PRI candidate will win the presidential election in the year 2000.

When Zedillo took office, his first major legislative initiatives were to alter the judicial system. The Supreme Court was changed to make it more independent and less responsive to the executive, and to give it responsibility to rule on the constitutionality of new laws.[9] Zedillo has made clear from his actions that he wishes to separate the presidency from governance of the PRI, although the party has been resistant to this. When the PRI held its National Assembly in September 1996, it refused to eliminate presidential involvement in the choice of the PRI candidate for president in 2000, despite Zedillo's preference to do so. The assembly reflected the PRI's uncertainty that future electoral victories would be automatic.

Mexico has long been an authoritarian nation. This is changing, but the process is arduous. Mexico, in the future, may change its current economic policy, but the status quo ante is dead. Mexico will surely change its political structure, and automatic PRI dominance is now a thing of the past. These changes coincide with the first three years of NAFTA. There may or may not be causation, but there surely is interaction between the political and the economic ferment.

Corruption

Although impossible to calculate, the impression exists within Mexico and among observers of the Mexican scene that corruption is more egregious there than in most other countries. The evidence is everywhere: presidents enriching themselves while in office; sinecures in state-owned enterprises for retiring politicians; padding and rigging of government procurement contracts; and squandering on white elephants much of the bonanza of oil revenues in the heady days of high prices during the 1970s. On a daily level, there is widespread mistrust of the police. Few Mexicans believe that there is equal justice under the law.

The economic opening limited some corruption opportunities. Once import licenses did not have to be obtained, and after the terms of foreign direct investment did not have to be minutely negotiated, illicit profits from these transactions were reduced. Privatization of government-owned enterprises limited the corruption inherent in providing jobs in them for favored politicians. These actions, however, left other forms of corruption untouched. In addition, the growing narcotics market opened new source of funds to practice corruption.

Each new president in recent years promised to reduce corruption, but by now the Mexican public is cynical. President Miguel De La Madrid's "moral renovation" renovated very little. The Salinas *sexenio*, following that of De La Madrid, did little more. The revelations about the illicit enrichment of Raúl Salinas, the ex-president's brother, have made clear that the fortunes that can be accumulated from a corrupt person close to the presidency are enormous. So far about $100 million in foreign bank accounts and property all over Mexico have been discovered in Raúl Salinas' name or under the account of *prestanombres*, literally, borrowed names; and the iceberg may be larger than this. Many police officers in Mexico City have been dismissed, and the army has been given a bigger role in law enforcement in the capital precisely to reduce corruption. The jury is still out on whether any of this will make much difference.

Other Bilateral Issues

The two issues that most aggravate relations between the United States and Mexico are the drug trade and migration. Each is highly complex, and although politicians use them to attack opponents, they cut across party lines and are not subject to sloganeering solutions. Each has the potential to explode at any time and overwhelm the progress made in fostering bilateral cooperation in other fields, from trade and investment to monetary matters.

Each is sometimes used to directly criticize NAFTA. The arguments are that increased Mexican exports to the United States facilitate the clandestine shipment of drugs in legitimate cargo, and that illegal immigrants are now more likely than ever to cross the border and then be used as *burros* to bring narcotics into the United States.[10] These are not serious anti-NAFTA arguments; if they were, all trade and migration would have to be reduced, and not just with Mexico because drug traders are not limited to basing their operations in any one country. They are arguments for greater vigilance as bilateral economic and human interactions increase, as one would wish them to do.

Migration

Many opponents of NAFTA argued that the agreement would stimulate emigration from Mexico to the United States; the main argument was that changes in Mexican agriculture would propel rural to urban migration within Mexico and across the border into the United States. This position had considerable resonance in California, both of whose federal senators opposed NAFTA on this score.

NAFTA does open Mexico to increased agricultural imports by reducing tariffs over a 15-year period for the most important crops, corn and beans. The shift in agricultural policy in Mexico is not, however, solely a NAFTA-stimulated phenomenon. Mexican authorities concluded independently that the benefits of producer subsidies that raised internal corn prices to double the world price were going to large commercial farmers and hardly at all to the subsistence farmers, who were leaving rural areas in any event. The old subsidy system was based on corn that producers placed into commerce, and subsistence farmers did little of this. The new structure, intended to be phased out over 15 years, is to provide subsidies based on income in order to target those who most need the government largesse. The old structure also impelled the government to provide consumer subsidies in the cities for corn products, particularly tortillas.

Beyond this, emigration from rural areas in Mexico is inevitable. The roughly 25 percent of Mexicans who live in rural areas contribute less than 10 percent of Mexico's GDP. In other words, they are largely impoverished and their school and health care facilities are inadequate. Rational and enterprising people will move in these circumstances. The issue here is not about NAFTA, but rather how successful Mexico can be in creating new jobs in both rural and urban areas, particularly the latter. NAFTA, as it supplements Mexico's macroeconomic policies, can contribute to this.

There is a long-term, short-term dichotomy. Emigration from Mexico will not slow down voluntarily unless incomes rise and Mexicans believe that growth will be maintained. This will take time—not an eternity, but at least a decade if all goes well. In the short term, the gradual rise in incomes is unlikely to deter would-be migrants. The effect of NAFTA on migration, therefore, is how much the policies embodied in the agreement can contribute to raising Mexican incomes, assuming that other economic and social policies move in the same stimulative direction.

The horizon of politicians tends to be short-term and they therefore seek quick solutions. These include building fences along the border, beefing up the presence of Border Patrol agents, and taking effective measures to punish employers who knowingly hire illegal immigrants. These measures were included in the immigration legislation approved in the final days of the Congress that adjourned in October 1996. They should have some short-term impact, but the record is not encouraging for sustained long-term results. Operation "Hold the Line," which augmented the Border Patrol presence in and around El Paso, Texas, seemed to discourage undocumented border crossers for a time, or at least encouraged them to seek other locations to enter the United States, but more recent data indicate that the deterrent effect may be diminishing.

The immigration issue did not arise out of NAFTA. Nor is it one that will be deeply affected by NAFTA in the short term. The salient question in the context of this study is whether the existence of NAFTA facilitates bilateral discussion on this issue or whether the United States would prefer to go it alone. The answer seems clear: cooperation generally on economic issues can only foster cooperation on migration matters.

The fact is that there has been more discussion between the two countries on migration matters during the past few years than had occurred during the previous 30 years taken together. During debates on earlier immigration legislation in the United States, particularly the Immigration Reform and Control Act (IRCA) of 1986, the Mexicans consciously refrained from giving any opinion. Today, there are regular consultations on the practices of both countries and a comprehensive binational study of the issue is under way.

What stimulated the change in Mexican tactics? Most of all, undoubtedly, was the realization that the United States was becoming more serious about stemming illegal immigration. The evidence from the past was that the United States passed laws to this effect, but then consciously refrained from enforcing them rigorously. But habits of consultation and discussion stemming from the negotiation and operation of NAFTA have had their influence as well. If NAFTA were now to disappear, it is highly probable that consultations on the immigration issue would cease. Consultation does not necessarily mean there will be solutions, certainly not on an issue as emotional and complex as migration. But without consultation, there can be no cooperative understandings.

Drug Traffic

The prevalent attitude in Mexico for many years was that the use of narcotics was a U.S. problem, and the issue was of secondary importance for Mexico. Cooperation between the two countries was at best asymmetrical under these circumstances. The Drug Enforcement Administration (DEA) operated in Mexico and there were joint efforts at drug interdiction. The Mexican authorities destroyed poppy and marijuana crops and seized many shipments of these drugs, methamphetamines, and cocaine transiting the country; but as long as consumption was not seen as a major domestic problem, the effort was not entered into enthusiastically. The government had to withstand considerable criticism that it was acting at the behest of the U.S. authorities, who were not doing enough themselves to deal with the trafficking and consumption problems.

This attitude changed in recent years as Mexico increasingly became a transit point and Mexican drug entrepreneurs began to carve out a position for themselves independent of the Colombia cartels. Drug use also rose within Mexico. The vast sums of money involved in the drug trade increasingly corrupted Mexican politics and the country's law-enforcement capacity. Mexico today is in danger of becoming a narco-democracy, if this has not already occurred. President Zedillo has said on many occasions that stemming the drug traffic and the lawlessness it has brought is Mexico's number one task.

As with migration, the issue here is whether the existence of NAFTA facilitates cooperation between the two countries in dealing with the drug trade. Had Mexico been decertified, as Colombia was in 1996, would this have induced more cooperation? My opinion is that decertification would have ended just about all anti-narcotic cooperation. Mexico is too proud a country, with too long a history of resentment about U.S. interference in its affairs, to have accepted U.S. decertification calmly. The political dynamic would not have permitted this.

With NAFTA in place, and efforts at closer bilateral relations sprouting across-the-board, the last thing the Mexican ties would wish is to contaminate all of this by conflic drug policy. The Mexican authorities leaned over backwards to deliver Juan García Abrego to the United States for trial (and conviction) on drug-related charges. Mexico declared him to be a U.S. citizen, which may or may not be the case, but used this argument to avoid having to defend the extradition of a Mexican, something that had no precedent in Mexico until recently.[11]

NAFTA does not deal with narcotics trade. But Mexico now has a self-interest in cooperating with the United States to reduce this trade and this interest is reinforced by the habits of cooperation that are becoming ever more pronounced under NAFTA.

Focusing on Key Issues

In an issue brief for the U.S. Congress, the Congressional Research Service highlighted the following bilateral matters:[12]

- trade;
- operation of the NAFTA supplemental agreements on the environment and labor;
- financial credits;
- immigration;
- drug trafficking;
- elections and political rights in Mexico; and
- allegations of human rights abuses in Mexico.

The list can be expanded to include economic policy in Mexico because this, even more than most items listed above, affects U.S. relations with its neighbor.

There is now an institutional structure for dealing with most of these issues, and there is considerably more dialogue on them today than in the years before NAFTA. To repeat a point made frequently in this study: Although dialogue does not necessarily resolve problems, there can be no resolution without dialogue. NAFTA has contributed immensely to making the U.S.-Mexican relationship more cooperative than was the case before the agreement came into the bilateral picture.

6

Conclusions

NAFTA is the most significant agreement between the United States and Mexico in this century. The agreement is intended to consolidate economic relations by providing a legal and institutional framework that had been lacking. Traders and investors in both countries can now have greater confidence in continuity of treatment—assurance on what the rules of the game will be—than existed earlier. The objectives of the agreement can be frustrated by internal and external shocks in each country, a stress in either on transitory internal politics over deepening the bilateral relationship, and wrong-headed domestic economic measures. For the first time in the two countries' modern relationship, however, the bricks and mortar for continued growth of bilateral economic activity are in place in a comprehensive, formal agreement.

Yet, while NAFTA provides a framework for *bilateral* U.S.-Mexican economic relations, it is not the dominant feature of *internal* developments in either country. These depend more on national economic policies and the nature and openness of their politics. The Mexican economy crashed in 1995 for reasons unrelated to NAFTA, but this had a major impact on the trade between the two countries. Mexico in recent years has gone through a political transformation that was unthinkable as few as 10 years ago, but any retrogression in this democratic opening would have serious, adverse repercussions on the bilateral relationship.

NAFTA cannot compensate for incorrect internal policies in either country, whether economic, political, or social, but it can augment the benefits of sound policy. This is more true for Mexico than for the United States. In 1995, Mexico's merchandise exports to the United States amounted to about 25 percent of its GDP, whereas U.S. merchandise exports to Mexico were less than 1 percent of U.S. GDP. The sheer size of the U.S. economy compared with that of Mexico—U.S. GDP is some 23 times greater than that of Mexico—in combination with the greater diversity of the U.S. export market, means that the potential benefits and losses of NAFTA are more important for Mexico.

Ten major conclusions can be reached based on the analysis in this progress report:

1. Under the main criterion that should be used to evaluate a trade agreement—namely, what is happening to trade?—NAFTA is performing as expected. Two-way trade is up and the rise is continuing. The type of industrial specialization that one hopes for in such an agreement in order to augment the competitiveness of companies is in fact taking place. This is evident from the growth of intra-industry trade.

2. The fear that free trade with Mexico would lead to a massive loss of jobs in the United States has turned out to be unfounded. To be sure, jobs have been lost as production and trade patterns have changed, but the overwhelming reality in the U.S. economy since NAFTA has been in existence is a massive increase in U.S. job-creation and, if anything, a shortage of qualified labor. U.S. monetary policy since 1994 has been designed to cool down economic and job growth in order to contain inflation; and NAFTA has been a sideshow, even a no-show, in this policy formulation.

3. Viewing the trade phenomenon from the Mexican side, the one bright feature of the Mexican economy during the collapse in the domestic market in 1995 was the increase in exports to the United States, which alleviated the extent of the depression. The Mexican economy is now recovering from that disastrous year, and so too are Mexican imports from the United States.

4. The trade patterns since NAFTA came into effect at the start of 1994 demonstrate clearly that tariff levels, when they are moderate, play a modest role in determining trade flows. The performance of the economy is far more important. A rich country draws in more imports than a poor one. A growing economy sucks in imports and a declining one dampens them. The U.S. economy has performed well during the three years of NAFTA and the United States has been a good market for Mexican goods and services. The Mexican economy drew in U.S. exports in 1994, when the economy was growing. U.S. exports declined in 1995, when the Mexican economy collapsed, and then grew again in 1996 as Mexico recovered positive economic growth.

5. U.S. exports to Mexico in 1995, even though they fell, were higher than they had been in 1993, the year before NAFTA came into effect. This is not intended to be a simple mercantilistic point, but rather to emphasize that the stabilization program pursued by Mexico to recover from the tragedy of 1995 did not unduly restrict two-way trade with the United States. Instead of relying on direct import restrictions, as had been its practice after previous downturns, this time Mexico relied on monetary, fiscal, and exchange-rate measures. The result was a smaller decline in U.S. exports to Mexico than after the 1982 economic collapse. The Mexican people endured great hardships in 1995, as they did after 1982, but the economic recovery was much more rapid this time.

6. The liaisons between Americans and Mexicans are growing in ways that never existed before. There are abundant links now between private actors, from business and nongovernmental organizations, and between officials of the two governments. Many of these new personal interactions were spawned by NAFTA. Dialogue does not necessarily resolve all problems, but lack of discussion is almost certain to allow problems to fester. This is surely the situation for such problems as environmental degradation, drug trafficking, and illegal immigration, all of which are now subjects of intense bilateral consultation.

7. Mexico, more than ever, is bombarded by U.S. values. Some of these, particularly the heightened consumerism more typical of the United States than of Mexico, are deplored by Mexican intellectuals. Others, such as an emphasis on transparency of economic and political measures and a stress on democratic values, surely are welcomed. The Mexican population has demonstrated over the past decade that it is willing to discard shibboleths that were paraded as verities when the changes promised economic improvement. Joining with the United States in NAFTA is the most prominent of these transformations. The perceived enemy became the main economic ally.

8. NAFTA is not like the European Union. There is no promise of economic and monetary union in North America. In one respect, however, there is some resemblance. European economic integration was seen by its founders as a way to diminish the hostility between Germany and France. Although there was no fear of war between Mexico and the United States, as there was in Europe, NAFTA is enveloping the two countries in more cooperative political relations than existed earlier.

9. NAFTA, in one respect, is working too well. The increase in cross-border competition is stimulating a protectionist backlash by affected producers in a number of key sectors. Internal

politics has led to some crass actions that run directly counter to competitive trade—these are evident in disputes over tomato and avocado trade, for example, and cross-border surface transportation. Trade conflicts are not new—in fact, they are probably less as a proportion of total trade than in the past—but the saving grace is that there are better dispute-settlement procedures in place than existed before NAFTA; and, as these become more embedded in practice over time, conflicts should be able to be resolved more quickly.

10. Three years is too short to assess the full impact of NAFTA. The agreement is designed to set in motion a period of adjustment in economic interactions between the two countries that is long-term in nature. The United States and Mexico are destined to be neighbors forever, as least for as long as the two countries exist—and the adjustment to this reality is a constant.

Finally, a statement rather than a conclusion. One should not lose sight of an elementary point that is often forgotten. An import duty is a tax on the consumer. If one believes in lower taxes, NAFTA moves modestly in this direction. If one believes in the importance of a competitive market, NAFTA encourages this. If one believes in consumer sovereignty, NAFTA stimulates this.

Notes

Chapter 1: Introduction

1. Public Citizen, "NAFTA's Broken Promises: The Border Betrayed," January 1996.

2. This uncertainty is made explicit in J. F. Hornbeck, "NAFTA, Mexican Trade Policy, and U.S.-Mexico Trade: A Longer-Term Perspective," Congressional Research Service, Library of Congress, March 11, 1996 (p. 1): "... it is worth reiterating that the benefits of freer trade are not measured by annual trade balances, but by broader economic changes that unfold over longer periods of time."

3. This is so even though the United States generally has a larger deficit in its merchandise trade with Canada than with Mexico. In 1994, the United States had a $14 billion merchandise trade deficit with Canada and a $1.3 billion surplus with Mexico. In 1995, the year of Mexico's severe economic decline, the balance with Mexico shifted to a deficit of $16 billion, while that with Canada was even larger, at $18 billion.

Chapter 2: How to Evaluate NAFTA

1. Mary Jane Bolle, "NAFTA: Estimates of Job Effects and Industry Trade Trends After Two Years," Congressional Research Service, Library of Congress, April 19, 1996.

2. J. F. Hornbeck, "NAFTA, Mexican Trade Policy, and U.S.-Mexico Trade: A Longer-Term Perspective," Congressional Research Service, Library of Congress, March 11, 1996, emphasizes this point in this report for the Congress. It would be helpful if more members of Congress would read the report.

3. This shift in emphasis can be seen in a series of NAFTA updates or snapshots, as they were called, from the U.S. Department of Commerce of February 1, 1995, September 26, 1995, and February 28, 1996. The September 26, 1995 report, "The Case for NAFTA," is the most ambitious of these in that it seeks to rebut anti-NAFTA arguments.

4. "NAFTAMATH—Two Years Later," talking points of the AFL-CIO Task Force on Trade, April 1996.

5. Technically, the United States cannot have a current account surplus as long as it saves less than it invests. The reason is that some of the invest-

ment must be financed by foreign savings. The U.S. savings rate is highly inadequate. In addition, as long as the public sector dis-saves, that is, has a deficit, this brings down the national savings rate. It is thus hard to make the case that a large budget deficit and a current account surplus are mutually consistent.

6. Gary Clyde Hufbauer and Kimberly Ann Elliott, *Measuring the Costs of Protection in the United States* (Washington, D.C.: Institute for International Economics, 1994), 11.

7. Federal Reserve Bank of Cleveland, *Economic Trends,* July 1996, 11.

8. Bolle, "NAFTA: Estimates of Job Effects," 2. Emphasis in original.

9. U.S. International Trade Commission, *Broom Corn Brooms,* Publication 2984, August 1996.

10. This technique for measuring the global welfare effects of economic integration is from Jacob Viner, *The Customs Union Issue* (Lancaster, Penn.: Lancaster Press for the Carnegie Endowment for International Peace, 1950).

11. United Nations Economic Commission for Latin America and the Caribbean (ECLAC), *Open Regionalism in Latin America and the Caribbean* (Santiago, Chile: ECLAC, 1994).

12. The particular column dealt with Turkey. Thomas L. Friedman, "Turkey Wings It," *New York Times,* July 17, 1996, sec. A, p. 23.

13. See Douglas A. Schuler, "The NAFTA and the Environment: Trade, Diplomacy, and Limited Protection," *International Trade Journal* 10, no. 3 (Fall 1996): 353–377.

14. The most critical publication on NAFTA's environmental record has been Public Citizen, "NAFTA's Broken Promises: The Border Betrayed," Public Citizen's Global Trade Watch, January 1996. The format of the document is to cite promises by President Clinton and other NAFTA supporters on environmental issues and then give specific examples of how they have not been met. Many of the anecdotes antedate NAFTA, and the central complaint is that the existence of NAFTA and related environmental agreements have done little or nothing to correct those.

15. If I may be permitted a personal note, when I held policy positions in the State Department until the mid-1970s, it was quite common to call my counterparts in Canada and Europe on monetary and trade matters. The same was true across the U.S. government. It never crossed my mind to do the same with Mexican officials. When it was necessary to speak officially, this was done exclusively through the Mexican embassy in Washington and the U.S. embassy in Mexico City. Direct conversations between U.S. and Mexican counterparts are now commonplace.

Chapter 3: Trade under NAFTA

1. Literally, the translation is "After this, therefore because of this." It is easy to show that both NAFTA proponents and opponents use this simplistic logic. Thus, in an information packet of August 1996 on NAFTA, USTR states: "During NAFTA's first two years, U.S. exports to our NAFTA part-

ners (Mexico and Canada) are up by 22 percent, or nearly $31 billion. . . ." In an anti-NAFTA publication by Sarah Anderson, John Cavanaugh, and David Ranney, (eds), "NAFTA's First Two Years: The Myths and Realities," Institute for Policy Studies and University of Illinois at Chicago, March 1996, the argument is made that the peso collapse in December 1994 "demonstrates not only the limitations of NAFTA, but the shortcomings of the entire approach to development that is being implemented in Mexico and throughout the hemisphere" (p. 1). Never mind that there were financial collapses before most of Latin American shifted its development approach and that many countries in the region are doing quite well economically under the current model.

2. Paul Krugman has written on the geography-trade relationship. See *Geography and Trade* (Cambridge, Mass.: MIT Press, 1991), and *Development, Geography, and Economic Theory* (MIT Press, 1995).

3. Mexico had leeway from the level of its bindings (ceilings it had agreed to in trade negotiations) in GATT to raise its duties without having to compensate other GATT members for this action, but neither NAFTA nor other free trade agreements that Mexico had entered into gave Mexico this option. Mexico, therefore, raised some consumer product duties against countries other than those with which it had free-trade agreements.

4. Interview with Sergio Muñoz, *Los Angeles Times*, September 15, 1996, section M, p. 3.

5. Opinion column by Sidney Weintraub, "The Death Rattles of a Monopoly," *Los Angeles Times*, September 29, 1996, section M, p. 1.

6. Chandler Stolp, "Quarterly U.S.-Mexican Trade Index," released each quarter in "Tracking U.S. Trade" by the Center for the Study of Western Hemispheric Trade, University of Texas at Austin.

7. David Gould, "Distinguishing NAFTA from the Peso Crisis," Federal Reserve Bank of Dallas, *Southwest Economy*, September-October 1996, pp. 6–10.

8. One has to be wary of the precision of reported FDI flows because they were often recorded for the wrong months and there was confusion between intended and actual flows. The system for obtaining FDI figures was therefore modified in 1995, as reported in the publication of the Mexican Investment Board, "Mexico Investment Update," second quarter 1996. The data come from the Bank of Mexico and INEGI, Mexico's statistical agency.

9. The quotation is from an article by Dan Balz on page 1 of the *Washington Post*, March 3, 1996.

10. The figures, based on U.S. Census Bureau data, are compiled by the Massachusetts Institute for Social and Economic Research (MISER). They are reported in a publication of the Washington, D.C., office of the United Nations Economic Commission for Latin America and the Caribbean (ECLAC), "NAFTA Implementation in the United States: The First Two Years," document LC/WAS/2.34, June 27, 1996.

11. The data in this paragraph are from U.S. Department of Commerce, *U.S. Foreign Trade Highlights 1995* (Washington, D.C.: U.S. Government

Printing Office, 1996), 142. SITC refers to Standard International Trade Classification.

12. Details on two-way trade broken down in a variety of ways can be found in Sidney Weintraub and Jan Gilbreath, "North American Trade Under NAFTA," NAFTA Effects Working Paper No. 2, Commission for Environmental Cooperation, Montreal, April 1996.

13. Sidney Weintraub, *NAFTA: What Comes Next?* (Westport, Conn.: Praeger for the Center for Strategic and International Studies, 1994), 45–46.

14. The breakdown is not always precise, but the data give a reliable indication of the kinds of goods that are being imported.

15. The data are from various issues of the monthly statistical publication *Indicadores Económicos* published by the Banco de México.

16. U.S. International Trade Commission (USITC), *Production Sharing: Use of U.S. Components and Materials in Foreign Assembly Operations, 1991–1994* (U.S. Imports Under Production Sharing Provisions of Harmonized Tariff Schedule Heading 9802), USITC publication 2966, May 1966, Washington, D.C.

17. Ibid., 2–4.

18. Pam Woodall, "The hitchhikers guide to cybernomics," survey article, *Economist*, September 28, 1996, 45.

19. These two rules are referred to as "NAFTA 'Lowlights'" in Gary Hufbauer and Jeffrey Schott, *NAFTA: An Assessment*, revised edition (Washington, D.C.: Institute for International Economics, 1993), 5–7. The same two authors have background discussions of these two industries in *North American Free Trade: Issues and Recommendations* (Washington, D.C.: Institute for International Economics, 1992).

20. The eight companies, in order of the quantity of vehicle sales in the wholesale market for January-May 1996, were Chrysler, General Motors, Ford, Volkswagen, Nissan, Mercedes-Benz, Honda, and BMW. This and other data in this paragraph are from the monthly publication of Grupo Financiero Bancomer, *Informe Económico*, Mexico City, July 1996.

21. The data were taken from BLS information dated July 9, 1996, on the Internet.

22. U.S. Department of Commerce, International Trade Administration, "Impact of the North American Free Trade Agreement on U.S. Automotive Exports to Mexico," Report to Congress, June 1996.

23. *Inside NAFTA*, September 4, 1996, pp. 11–12, from the U.S. Department of Commerce report to Congress, "Impact of the North American Free Trade Agreement on U.S. Automotive Exports to Mexico," August 1996.

24. Perhaps the explanation needs a bit more elaboration. If the fabric is U.S.-formed and U.S.-cut, apparel imports from Mexico can enter the United States under what is called "special regime," that is, without quota and without duty. These are 807A imports. If they are U.S.-cut but are not U.S.-formed, the apparel that comes in is known as 807 imports and the duty must be paid on the value added in Mexico. The 807 imports are subject to the U.S. quota for Mexico only if the fabric is non-NAFTA in origin. Mexico-formed fabrics pay the regular duty and are subject to the regular quota if the fabric is of non-NAFTA origin. Even though the old 807 category for the value-added, production-sharing tariff treatment (see the maquiladora discussion in this section) has been changed to 9802 under the U.S. harmonized tariff structure, the textile trade still refers to 807 and 807A.

25. News article by Robin Bulman, *Journal of Commerce*, September 24, 1996, p. 1A.

26. The list is based on U.S. Trade Representative, *Foreign Trade Barriers* (Washington, D.C.: U.S. Government Printing Office, 1996).

27. I can vouch for this from my own experience at Mexican marketplaces.

28. Much of this information was developed from discussions with U.S. officials in USTR and the Department of Commerce.

29. The one case that I know of from personal involvement was that of J.C. Penney, which was forced to delay the launching of a number of stores in Mexico after substantial sums already had been invested.

30. UN ECLAC, "NAFTA Implementation in the United States," 22.

31. The practices of all three NAFTA countries are reviewed in Beatriz Leycegui, William Robson, and S. Dahlia Stein, *Trading Punches: Trade Remedy Law and Disputes Under NAFTA* (Washington, D.C.: National Planning Association, 1995).

32. UN ECLAC, "NAFTA Implementation in the United States," 22.

33. It will be harder, but not impossible, to apply this same logic to the treatment of CVD cases so long as governments have the independence to subsidize exports.

34. Armand Peschard-Sverdrup, "The U.S.-Mexico Fresh Winter Tomato Trade Dispute: The Broader Implications," Center for Strategic and International Studies, Washington, D.C., September 1996. Peschard-Sverdrup's conclusion was supported in an article in the *Wall Street Journal*, April 3, 1996, p. 1, written by Helene Cooper and Bruce Ingersoll, which had the following headline: "With Little Evidence, Florida Growers Blame Tomato Woes on Nafta."

35. USITC, *Fresh Tomatoes and Bell Peppers*, Investigation No. TA-201–66, publication 2985, August 1986, p. I–3. USITC, in its report, points out that in an investigation under section 202 of the Trade Act of 1974, three criteria must be met: (1) imports are entering in increased quantities; (2) the domestic industry is seriously injured or threatened with serious injury; and (3) the increased imports are a substantial cause of the actual or threatened serious injury. The commissioners did not so find.

36. USTR press release containing the joint statement of Ambassador Barshefsky and Secretary Kantor regarding the ITC decision on tomatoes, July 2, 1996.

37. David E. Sanger, "President Wins Tomato Accord for Floridians," *New York Times*, October 12, 1996.

38. *Journal of Commerce*, October 10, 1996, p. 7A, article by Kevin G. Hall, "California trade official raps Clinton on Mexico," with a subhead, "State trade and commerce secretary scolds the administration over failure to open up the trucking sector."

39. *Inside NAFTA,* "USDA action to leave avocado ban in place for another year," September 4, 1996, p. 1.

Chapter 4: Finance

1. Subcomandante Marcos of the EZLN made this point explicitly.

2. Andres Oppenheimer, *Bordering on Chaos* (Boston: Little, Brown & Co., 1996) has much informative discussion of the Zapatista grievances and the subsequent behavior of the movement.

3. Banco de México, *Informe Anual 1994*, 60. Reserve data given later in this chapter come from the same source.

4. Oppenheimer, *Bordering on Chaos*, gives ample details for those interested.

5. The Bank of Mexico goes to pains to point this out in its 1994 annual report, citing the current account deficits of Singapore, Malaysia, and Thailand over a number of years (p. 47).

6. A mainstream judgment about the success of the loan can be found in Bradford De Long, Christopher De Long, and Sherman Robinson, "The Case for Mexico's Rescue," *Foreign Affairs* 75, no. 3 (May/June 1996): 8–14. Thomas L. Friedman, in a column in the *New York Times* on September 25, 1996, reached the same conclusion. A letter to the editor by Jerome I. Levinson on September 30, in response to Friedman's column, argued that the burden of adjustment in the Mexican economy was borne by the workers.

7. The data are extracted from reports by Mexico's National Statistical Institute (INEGI). The underemployment measure used covers those persons who were forced to work less than 35 hours a week for market reasons or who worked more than 40 hours for less than the minimum wage.

Chapter 5: Institutions and Interactions

1. The Bank of Montreal, one of two Canadian banks that have entered the Mexican market, makes much of the fact that it now operates in all three countries. For one result of this three-country activity, see Bank of Montreal, "Business Executives' Views of NAFTA Two Years Later," findings of a survey of 250 executives in the United States, Canada, and Mexico, 1996.

2. The validity of this statement is supported by the survey findings of the Bank of Montreal.

3. A description of NAFTA provisions for resolving disputes can be found in International Division, U.S. Chamber of Commerce (CoC), *A Guide to the North American Free Trade Agreement: What it Means for U.S. Business* (Washington, D.C.: CoC, 1992), 70–75.

4. Public Citizen, "NAFTA's Broken Promises: The Border Betrayed," Public Citizen's Global Trade Watch, January 1996.

5. This is from "Mexico and NAFTA Report," September 26, 1996, published weekly in London by Latin American Newsletters.

6. CEC, "Weighing the Values of Trade and the Environment under the NAFTA and the NAAEC," 1996.

7. The paid-in capital is $225 million from each country and the callable capital is $1.275 billion from each country over four years.

8. U.S. General Accounting Office (GAO), "Environmental Infrastructure Needs in the U.S.-Mexican Border Region Remain Unmet," GAO-RCED-96–179, July 1996.

9. Roderic Ai Camp, "The Zedillo Legacy," policy paper, Center for Strategic and International Studies, October 3, 1996.

10. John Sweeney makes these points in an article on what he considers to be the failing U.S. drug policy in Latin America. John Sweeney, "In Latin America: Quelling Chaos," *Foreign Service Journal* 73, no. 10 (October 1996): 34–39.

11. Sam Dillon, "Mexico Quietly Makes Big Shifts Toward a More Pro-U.S. Policy," *New York Times*, May 2, 1996, p. 1.

12. Larry K. Storrs, "Mexican-U.S. Relations: Issues for the 104th Congress," Congressional Research Service, Library of Congress, July 15, 1996.

Bibliography

American Textile Manufacturers Institute. *Textile Highlights.* March 1996.

——. *Economic Developments in the Textile Industry.* June 1996.

Anderson, Sarah, John Cavanaugh, and David Ronney, eds. "NAFTA's First Two Years: The Myths and the Realities." Institute for Policy Studies and University of Illinois at Chicago, March 1996.

Bank of Montreal. "Business Executions: Views of NAFTA Two Years Later." *Findings of Survey of 250 Executives in the United States, Canada, and Mexico.* 1996.

Bolle, Mary Jane. "NAFTA: Estimates of Job Effects and Industry Trade Trends After Two Years." Congressional Research Service, Library of Congress, April 19, 1996.

Camp, Roderick Ai. "The Zedillo Legacy." Center for Strategic and International Studies, March 1996.

Commission for Environmental Cooperation. "Dispute Avoidance: Weighing the Values of Trade and the Environment under the NAFTA and the NAAEC." 1996

DeLong, Bradford, Christopher DeLong, and Sherman Robinson. "The Case for Mexico's Rescue." *Foreign Affairs* 75, no 3 (1996): 8–14.

Economist. September 28, 1996. "The Hitchhiker's Guide to Cybernomics."

Grupo Financiero Bancomer. *Informe Económico.* July 1996.

Hornbeck, J.F. "NAFTA, Mexican Trade Policy, and U.S.-Mexico Trade: A Longer-Term Perspective." Congressional Research Service, Library of Congress, March 11, 1996.

Hufbauer, Gary Clyde, and Kimberly Ann Elliott. *Measuring the Costs of Protection in the United States.* Washington, D.C.: Institute for International Economics, 1994.

Hufbauer, Gary C., and Jeffrey J. Schott. *North American Free Trade: Issues and Recommendations.* Washington, D.C.: Institute for International Economics, 1992.

———. *NAFTA: An Assessment.* Washington, D.C.: Institute for International Economics, 1993.

Inside NAFTA. September 4, 1996, pp. 11–12.

Journal of Commerce. September 24, 1996, sec. A, p. 1. Bulman, Robin, "Apparel Workers Stranded as Plant Moves to Mexico."

———. October 10, 1996, sec. A, p. 7. Hall, Kevin G, "California Trade Official Raps Clinton on Mexico."

Krooth, Richard. *Mexico, NAFTA and the Hardships of Progress: Historical Patterns and Shifting Methods of Oppression.* Jefferson, N.C. and London: McFarland & Co., 1995.

Krugman, Paul. *Geography and Trade.* Cambridge, Mass.: MIT Press, 1991.

———. *Development, Geography, and Economic Theory.* Cambridge, Mass: MIT Press, 1995.

Leycegui, Beatriz, William Robson, and S. Dahlia Stein. *Trading Punches: Trade Remedy Law and Disputes Under NAFTA.* Washington, D.C.: National Planning Association, 1995.

Los Angeles Times. September 15, 1996, sec. M, p. 3. Sergio Muñoz interview with President Ernesto Zedillo

———. September 29, 1996. sec. M, p. 1. "The Death Rattles of a Monopoly."

Mexican Investment Board. "Mexico Investment Update." Second quarter 1996.

Mexico and NAFTA Report. Latin American Newsletters, London, September 26, 1996.

New York Times. May 2, 1996, p. 1. Dillon, Sam, "Mexico Quietly Makes Big Shifts Toward a More Pro-U.S. Policy."

———. July 17, 1996, sec. A, p. 23. Friedman, Thomas L., "Turkey Wings It."

———. October 12, 1996, p. 1. Sanger, David E., "President Wins Tomato Accord for Floridians."

Office of the U.S. Trade Representative. *Foreign Trade Barriers.* Washington, D.C.: U.S. Government Printing Office, 1996.

———. Joint statement of Ambassador Barshefsky and Commerce Secretary Kantor regarding ITC decision on tomatoes. July 2, 1996.

———. "North American Free Trade Agreement Information Package." August 1996.

Oppenheimer, Andres. *Bordering on Chaos*. Boston: Little, Brown & Co., 1996.

Peschard-Sverdrup, Armand. "The U.S.-Mexico Fresh Winter Tomato Trade Dispute: The Broader Implications." Center for Strategic and International Studies, September 1996.

Public Citizen. "NAFTA's Broken Promises: The Border Betrayed." Public Citizen's Global Trade Watch, January 1996.

Schuler, Douglas A. "The NAFTA and the Environment: Trade, Diplomacy, and Limited Protection." *International Trade Journal* 10, no. 3 (1996): 353–377.

Stolp, Chandler, and Sidney Weintraub. "NAFTA: Challenges and Opportunities for a 21st-Century Texas." *Lyceum* 10 (Spring/Summer 1993): 16–23.

Storrs, K. Larry. "Mexico-U.S. Relations: Issues for the 104th Congress." Congressional Research Service, Library of Congress, July 15, 1996.

Sweeney, John. "In Latin America: Quelling Chaos." *Foreign Service Journal* 76, no. 10 (1996): 34–39.

United Nations Economic Commission for Latin American and the Caribbean (ECLAC). *Open Regionalism in Latin America and the Caribbean*. Santiago, Chile: ECLAC, 1994.

———. "NAFTA Implementation in the United States: The First Two Years." Document LC/WAS/L.34, June 27, 1996.

U.S. Chamber of Commerce, International Division. *A Guide to the North American Free Trade Agreement: What it Means for U.S. Business*. Washington, D.C.: Chamber of Commerce, 1992.

U.S. Department of Agriculture. *Effects of the North American Free Trade Agreement on U.S. Agricultural Commodities*. Economic Research Service, March 1993.

———. *NAFTA: Year Two and Beyond*. Report by the NAFTA Economic Monitoring Task Force., April 1996.

U.S. Department of Commerce, International Trade Administration. "Impact of the North American Free Trade Agreement on U.S. Automotive Exports to Mexico." Report to Congress, June 28, 1996.

———. "The Case for NAFTA." September 26, 1996.

U.S. General Accounting Office. "Environmental Infrastructure Needs in the U.S.-Mexican Border Region Remain Unmet." Washington, D.C.: GAO/RCED (July 1996), 96–179.

U.S. International Trade Commission. *Fresh Tomatoes from Mexico.* Investigation no. 731–TA–747 (Preliminary), Publication 2967, May 1996.

———. *Production Sharing: Use of U.S. Components and Materials in Foreign Assembly Operations, 1991–1994.* U.S. Imports Under Production Sharing Provisions of Harmonized Tariff Schedule Heading 9802. Washington, D.C.: USITC 2966, May 1996.

———. *Broom Corn Brooms.* Publication 2984, August 1996.

———. *Fresh Tomatoes and Bell Peppers.* Investigation no. TA–201–66, Publication 2985, August 1996.

Viner, Jacob. *The Customs Union Issue.* Lancaster, Penn.: Lancaster Press for the Carnegie Endowment for International Peace, 1950.

Washington Post, March 3, 1996, p. 1. Balz, Dan, "Dole Wins Decisively in South Carolina Primary."

Weintraub, Sidney. *NAFTA: What Comes Next?* Westport, Conn.: Praeger for the Center for Strategic and International Studies, 1994.

Weintraub, Sidney, and Jan Gilbreath. "North American Trade Under NAFTA." Commission for Environmental Cooperation. NAFTA Effects Working Paper no. 2, April 1996.

Index

About the Author

Sidney Weintraub holds the William E. Simon Chair in Political Economy at the Center for Strategic and International Studies and is Professor Emeritus at the Lyndon B. Johnson School of Public Affairs of the University of Texas at Austin. A career diplomat in the U.S. Department of State from 1949 to 1975, Dr. Weintraub held the post of deputy assistant secretary of state for international finance and development from 1969 to 1974 and assistant administrator of the U.S. Agency for International Development in 1975. He was also a senior fellow at the Brookings Institution.

He is the sole author or editor of some 20 books and more than 130 articles. Recent titles include *NAFTA: What Comes Next?* (Praeger, for CSIS, 1994); *A Marriage of Convenience: Relations between Mexico and the United States* (Oxford University Press, 1990); "U.S. Foreign Policy and Mexican Immigration," in *At the Crossroads: Mexico and U.S. Immigration Policy* (Rowman and Littlefield, 1997), for which he was a coeditor; and "NAFTA and U.S. Economic Sovereignty," in *NAFTA and Sovereignty: Trade-offs for Canada, Mexico, and the United States* (CSIS, 1996), which he also coedited. Dr. Weintraub received a master's degree in economics at Yale University and his Ph.D. in economics at American University.